LETTERS OF THE

SCATTERED BROTHERHOOD

IF therefore ye are intent upon wisdom a lamp will not be wanting and a shepherd will not fail, and a fountain will not dry up.

ANONYMOUS

LETTERS OF THE
SCATTERED BROTHERHOOD

Edited by
MARY STRONG

"Walk in immortality now."

HARPER & BROTHERS PUBLISHERS

New York and London

LETTERS OF THE SCATTERED BROTHERHOOD

I-Y

PREFACE

THE Letters of the Scattered Brotherhood have been published in a religious weekly during the past fourteen years. The editor of the magazine once wrote in reply to questions concerning their origin, "They are letters of genuine spiritual experience; they are not contributions written for a journal" nor are they written by one person as was suggested because of the likeness of the terminology in many of them. The language common to all of them has been used down the ages in the endeavor to find words to describe and convey the meaning of meditation and spiritual awareness. Anonymity has been preserved for the reason that with contemporary material of this kind it has been thought wise to keep the spiritual significance free from personal association.

The quotations have been included as evidence of the timelessness of the idea of inner spiritual illumination and of the great company scattered the world over without regard to space, time, age or creed, who have found faith to walk in immortality now.

M. S.

LETTERS OF THE

SCATTERED BROTHERHOOD

If any man will do His will, he shall know of the doctrine. . . . and ye shall know the truth, and the truth shall make you free.

St. John, Chaps. 7 and 8

L ET US CONSIDER AGAIN WHAT OUR DAILY LIVING IS, THIS human living without thought; the conduct of people, the philosophy needed to live upon earth, to live intelligently, the mystery of pleasure and pain. First it appears that we are spoiled from lack of discipline, self-discipline. We are ignorant, too, and full of wild emotions, savage dislikes, greed, pride; pride of family, of race, community and nation.

This emotional fever-bag is our danger, for left to itself, inflated by angry argument, it is destructive and overpowers the balance of clear thinking. Through it we are influenced and swayed by passing events, the daily news and all the harm of misinformation. When possessed by states that are ungoverned, even while we carry our outward poise, there is a kind of lawlessness that swings to inertia, a what's-the-use attitude of mind, a refusal to make an effort which is a kind of lawlessness also. A child asks, Why is it necessary to have law and discipline? Because it is needful to establish a balanced order of conduct. Think for a moment of yourselves as raw material; through your acceptance or rejection of a thought, an idea, you establish your lives, your individualities. Emotion is as wild and unpredictable as the weather and must be faced and dominated. No wonder the ancients called it the devil, for at times it will run away with you, weaken your resolves, loosen your armor and plunge you into hell. Here is where pain often comes in and is indeed the drill sergeant. You have seen how many wild natures have been touched and softened by pain and sorrow. But why go that way to illumination? You who have started on this strange and beautiful journey, who have sensed immortality and touched it, have opened a door into a place where the mystery of life will be simplified for you if you will obey these promptings from within.

1

For many this is beyond understanding and they seek the satisfaction of penance in sacrifice and good works. That is not to be condemned, but it is only the first step, for as was said by one who lived in the thirteenth century, "Visible deeds do not increase the goodness of the inner life, however long and broad, whatever their number or dimension; its goodness is its own. The visible deeds of virtue can never be worth much *if* the inward process is small or has little life; but they never can be of little worth if the inner life is rich and great. The inner life goes on perpetually and draws upon God, from the very heart of Him, for the inner life of a man is His son."

Therefore obey the promptings that come to you from within when you have true communion with him, and you will learn your requirements, your disciplines, renunciations as well as illumination and the peace that passeth all understanding. With this knowledge you will find that it will be very uncomfortable for you if you get out of balance. This power held in stillness will go far toward stopping wars, for it will indeed move mountains and bring order out of chaos, as it is a living force. If you believe that character can be changed and transmuted, act on the promise. For to be freed from the laws of the material world we must pay the price, and the price is to make this instrument clean, pure, steady, vigilant, strong and faithful in little things.

Come closer to the center of all light; come freed from the ignorant emotional habits, from subtle appetites of prejudice and criticism. More is told you than by spoken words; only make way for the Light and you will be oriented and held in safety and great will be the results in your day, your hours, your seconds of time. The mystery of living will then be revealed to you . . . it is the transmutation of this living entity into the divine spiritual Man.

> *That which is now called the Christian religion*
> *existed among the ancients, and never did not exist*
> *from the planting of the human race until Christ*
> *came in the flesh, at which time the true religion*
> *which already existed began to be called Christianity.*
>
> *(Nam res ipsa quae nunc Christiana religio nucu-*
> *patur, erat & apud antiquos, nec defuit ab initio*
> *generis humani, quousque ipse Christus veniret in*
> *carna, unde vera religio quae iam erat, coepit appel-*
> *lari Christiana.)*
>
> St. Augustine, *Opera*, Basileae, 1569

YES, IT IS ALWAYS MORE OR LESS THE SAME PROBLEM, THAT of dealing with states of mind, and as we have told you before, they are nothing but challenging thoughts rearing up to attack you. When we first told you that all things human can be resolved to thought you received an intellectual perception; you perceived also that when your mind is tempted from its spiritual center your defenses are lowered and you automatically allow the outer you to have more freedom than is his right. Now that you have come into a small degree of realization of this truth there is still a tonal recollection of the fear contained in the old thoughts and that fear lies heavy on the spirit. Try to throw all that into the limbo where it belongs, give it no fastening room; it will then clutch emptiness and be swept away. Your task is to remain eternally unshaken within, to meet untoward states with what we have called action-thought. Heavenly thought is divine order; it is clean, it is joy, serenity and peace, and it will bring about your victory; no more to rear in anxious thought or chaotic emotion. Let them fall off like the dreary bundle they are and step forward in divine manhood.

In human relations refrain from the luxury of emotional storms of resentments and "righteous" indignation. There is no righteousness in emotional violence, and if you are assailed in the shadowy night when your armor is loosened, pray simply, as you did when you were a child, for has it not been written, "The entrance of thy words giveth light"?

The task for this period is not to let uncreative thought have lodging room. You say you make pictures, your mind conceives them like dark magic. Try not to do this, and the best way not to make negative pictures is to make spiritual pictures. Let into your mind the noble company of thoughts, thus will you keep out the rabble. Make your mental company glorious.

I understand your dilemma. The mind grows tired of one thing, and once it tires and dries up you must have a bright new toy to catch the careering mind and give it fresh comfort. You are not alone in this. The stream of consciousness is often like a disorder; a fumbling, a groping of the human race, is this formless thinking. The great ones have left many guideposts and I will recall one to you: "Thou wilt keep him in perfect peace whose mind is *stayed* on thee." Be careful not to misunderstand this and sink into solemnity which can become melancholy. Do not strain at gnats; release others, release yourself, be gay, be reborn, be refreshed!

And the Voice went forth throughout the world . . .
and each one heard it according to his capacity; old
men and youths and boys and sucklings and women:
the Voice was to each one as each one had the power
to receive it.

Shemoth [R.c.v.]

IN THIS JOURNEY YOU HAVE SET OUT UPON, YOU PLAY A DUAL
role, you are both doctor and patient. You are both human
and spiritual, wise and foolish, good and bad, civilized and
savage. There are those who say there is no evil. Let us not be
confused for there are subtle contradictions that lead to
trouble. "In *him* there is no variableness neither shadow of
turning," *he* is the light in whom there is no darkness at all;
but where light is not, where destructive human emotions are
in control, there is the manifestation of darkness, there is human savagery, there is chaos. When the individual wakes to the
knowledge that God is to be known and turns his face toward
light he takes the first step toward realization of his godhood;
with faith as his shield, the sword of the Spirit in his hand and
the spurs of resolution on his feet, he presses on to his fulfillment as a son of God. This is the way to become reborn, the
opportunity our human birth has given us. And it is not wise
ever to underestimate the strength of our enemy, the prejudices, weaknesses and fearfulness of the human self. We will
not suffer such dismay if we know we have them to deal with.
But do not give these emotions power over you by dwelling on
them in morbid discouragement. This is where you are doctor
as well as patient, and awareness of the Love of the indwelling
Christ is the medicine, it is the antidote, it is the healing of
the Spirit; abide in it, for of yourself you can do nothing and
in him all things are possible.

In the human experience are warring natures, hot fermenta-
tions, old doubts and cynicisms, the soul sicknesses from which
you can be freed if you will set your heart upon him. His
healing balsam is Love, it is given you to compound, it cannot
be thrust upon you.

May the Lord of all, the very real and present Saviour, the

very quick, the very vital, breathe his health in you and fill you with divine breath; may he hold your mind in stillness, quicken your thoughts, speak with your tongue and listen with your ear; may he give you the impulse of the moment that you may hold it, illumined.

One has said, "This is no voyage for a little barque, this which my venturesome prow goes cleaving, nor for a pilot who would spare himself." And yet today when the earth is more greatly troubled than ever before, whole communities of people turn their faces away from their responsibility to a world in peril. In their daily lives, where vigilance should begin, they cling to habits of comfort and self-indulgence, eyes dull, ears stopped, inertia and indifference like chains upon their feet. At no time is this voyage for a pilot who would spare himself, for his soul's sake, for his beloved's sake, and for the sake of his country.

This is a solemn time, for which you have been gently prepared. Keep in the simple path, keep in the Word and it will set you free. And by that is meant that you should be valiant in your insistence upon keeping aware so that you hear the voice within, that the Word may abide in you and in the midst of confusion keep your spirit in peace. This is your role, this is your great service to mankind. Let "I am the Light of the world within thee!" be your battle cry.

> *Have you anything more important to do? Ask yourself that question when interruptions threaten and you are tempted to set this hour aside. . . . It is not a futile task. Once the inter-relation of all created things is even dimly sensed, one cannot be small. The mantle of magnitude is over the most humble part of the whole.*
>
> Betty White

THE REASON THE WORLD IS IN THIS STATE IS BECAUSE IT HAS not been alert, awake, vigilant in obeying the words of the Spirit. Hate, the negations, the antitheses of the Spirit, have been vigilant; the negatives always are. You have been more awake because you disciplined yourselves within; because you sought and found. But your scale is much too small where it should be higher in its vigilance and this is the reason you feel the outside pressure as much as you do and find it so difficult to withstand. This awareness of God must be fiery; you must be ablaze with it, for then it will be felt and the picture of this glory will be translated now, this minute, into a welling up of faith and power. You know that much of your trouble is due to your own inertias. In spite of them, think what a gift you have with which to face this crisis. Every waking moment stand in God's presence with him in your heart. In quiet and confidence is your strength, and from now on, when you go out into life do not go in your human dignities, but go as an ambassador of God, that through your abiding in him you may translate his words into daily living. Through your quiet communions you will be given humility and power, for you can offer yourself as a living channel for him to pour through his healing wisdom; "I will not leave you comfortless, I will come to you." Accept this divine gift wholeheartedly. There are those who cry out, "Why does God allow these things to be?" Do we allow him his way with us? If you choose you can join the army of spiritual soldiers, marching invincible, in an invisible world, in immortality now.

. . . Much depends upon making up your mind. The nature of the human animal, as you well know, is subject to suggestion; the feeling-nature, when left to human devices, is unprotected, easily dismayed, elated, bored, irritated. The mind is moved by noises, cold, heat, stupidities, a letter, the disloyalty of a friend. But when the mind is made up, all these challenges can be divinely met; you are not defenseless. You are only defenseless when you are spiritually asleep. Bring into focus your godhood, your divine manhood by saying, "I make up my mind to be in the light of faith always, while I talk to people, while I walk, while I eat, Wherever I go, into every house. I will use it against all alarms, I will dwell in his eternal patience, in God's name I will be reborn!"

Because God made not death; neither delighteth He when the living perish. For He created all things that they might have being; and the generative powers of the world are healthsome and there is no poison of destruction in them, nor hath hades royal dominion upon earth,—for righteousness is immortal.

                                              Wisdom of Solomon

For one soul that exclaims, "Speak Lord, for thy servant heareth," there are ten that say, "Hear Lord! for Thy servant speaketh," and there is no rest for these.

                                              Pamela Grey

SOMEONE SAID LONG AGO, "RELIGION IS NOT A MELANCHOLY; the Spirit of God is not a dampe!" We have told you many times to keep from any tendency toward sadness, resignation and melancholy in your lives; the spirit must never be resigned nor melancholy nor gloat upon sorrow, which in some, unfortunately, is associated with a spiritual way of life. If the Spirit is real it is joy in essence, it is peace and faith. Now faith, divine faith, is an illumined state, it challenges everything mortal with a confident joy; indeed I would like to use the word merriment instead of joy here, as in the old English song, "God rest you merry, gentlemen; let nothing you dismay!" Yes, the world is sad, tragic and the suffering terrible. But we have been shown how in such times we must and can be gallant and to be gallant is to be joyous and to have true joy we must have faith. The kingdom of heaven is happiness because those who have found it and abide in it have become aware of the beauty of the infinite Spirit. Those who live in that kingdom know that everything must be met and challenged with a shout; challenge everything with the Spirit of joy. This may seem a hard saying for it seems to leave out pity. No, the lifting quality of confidence, of faith in ultimate victory, heals, sustains and comforts those in darkness and sorrow. If you can keep your inspiration gaily, confidently, many of the discouraging human attributes will be purified. The secret is—and this is what you are here for—to find the pearl of great price, to keep from losing it, from letting it grow dull and to remember that it has the power to release you from those characteristics which have held you a prisoner to your own limitations. This is being on the side of the angels.

The Eternal is good to those who wait for him, to a soul who seeks him. It is good to wait in silence for the help of the Eternal; let a man sit alone in silence, since it is the Eternal's hand.

Lamentations, Chap. 2 [Moffatt]

IN THESE DAYS OF STRAIN BEWARE OF THE EMOTIONS THAT ARE hosts to violence, for they lead to sorrow. Silence is your role. It isn't that we ask you to keep out of the arena but it is necessary to wear the armor of God when you are in it. If you would bring victory for goodness and order and peace, be a

channel for the omnipotent Spirit to flow through and do the
work in splendor. Watch your human weaknesses that frustrate
and clog the channel. Be on guard and keep in the invisible
remembering that of yourselves you can do nothing, the
Father within doeth the work.

I will make a picture for you which may be helpful.

You close your eyes to the outside world. Think of yourself,
your mind, as a shining surface within a circle that can contract and grow small or expand and grow larger, smooth and
glowing. A thought, like a speck of dust, floats down, touches
the surface and immediately the surface contracts to a pin point
and is concerned with a fear in that speck of thought. Hot
cinders of irritation lodge on this smooth surface of content
and happiness; the circle contracts and the cinder seems to
become a mountain in proportion to the surface, and fills your
whole conscious life. To perfect the reality of your daily life
you are to remove the cinders, the specks of dust, the hot ashes
of emotion, by illuminating this surface in the circle until it
consumes all foreign matter which these thoughts personify,
and the secret is the instant attack. Your creative thought,
sublimated by imagination, will transmute and dispel the fears,
the reactions to human duplicities and betrayals that so vio-
lently irritate the surface and involuntarily hold your attention.

There; it's a clumsy metaphor. But what we are trying to tell
you is that by overcoming through awareness, by abstinence
and being free from anything that binds or enslaves, you keep
your circle shining and wide as the universe. But be aware, be
aware of your tongue's betrayal, of thoughts that enfeeble you.
Shake off these things which are appetites in strange disguises,
that you may be a channel for power to pour through you to
the human race. Keep the surface of this circle within you free
from dust and cinders that come to contract your glory into
littleness.

It is difficult when the outside is hard pressed by the trouble in the world to keep the inside serene, but it is only difficult when you think that *you* can make it serene. The serenity will be given you; that is the benediction and the reward for those who sought and knocked and found. You are here at this moment, at this time, at this place, in this Presence and the Presence is the only Reality, and he is thy shepherd.

> *Simple said, I see no danger; Sloth said, Yet a little more sleep: and Presumption said, Every vat must stand upon his own bottom. And so they lay down to sleep again, and Christian went on his way.*
>
> *Pilgrim's Progress*

NOT LONG AGO A STATEMENT FOR FAITH IN ACTION WAS GIVEN to one whose daily work is complicated by harassing personalities, perhaps one of the most difficult tests of character for all of us. I quote it for you: "Say to yourself, 'I will keep all controversial opinion, all human impulses and talk *without* myself, in the outer realm of my life, for I know that trial and error, failures and half successes, the onslaught of personalities, obstinacies both within and without my own personality, are the passing and changing elements of living. I shall keep them outside the walls of my fortress. I know that within me in the quietness beyond silence, is the assurance of immortal life and the potentiality for peace here and now. I know by this act, this sacrament of communion with the divine Presence within me, I am being freed from those responses and impulses that would keep me earth bound. I know that as I live this life it is but an echo as compared to the Life within, eternal, immortal, omniscient.' Take strength, my daughter, from these words, for they will be a healing breath to your body and they are protection to your mind. Go about thy work serene and free."

To another was said: "Receive the assurance of your protection; know with confidence that gentleness within is your strength. The immediate dismays and obstacles are apt to blind us from seeing our objectives. Do not bruise yourself against a stone wall, and do not ask why, because the knowledge needful is given you step by step, and what is most needful at this measured moment in your time, is that you realize your protection through a gentle spirit within yourself, that you are aware of this and keep faith in the invisibility of the Holy Ghost, the glory of the great and good peace of your inner self. Go thy way, knowing. The reason so many are cynical in the confusions and alarms is because the wrongs are being worked out; they make the noise in the world, the tragic sound that brings sudden terror and dismay. The very quietness of goodness is undramatic and therefore too often unseen. You have a part to play, every living soul has a part to play. So do not forget your special role and do not underestimate the unseen influence of a son of God. Abide in His words and go thy way in peace."

> *Hope holds to Christ the mind's own mirror out*
> *To take His lovely likeness more and more.*
>   . . .
> *There is your world within.*
> *There rid the dragons, root out the sin*
> *Your will is law in that small commonweal.*

Gerard Manley Hopkins, 1844-1889

∽

WHEN YOU HAVE REACHED A NEW AND HIGHER PLANE OF spiritual awareness remember that with it comes the challenge to abide there. The experience of deeper peace and joy is apt to carry with it what we may call personal confidence as well as a more profound realization that it has been a gift of the spirit, the inevitable reward of aspiration and holy intent. Your work is to guard it, like country newly won, so that it will not be retaken by the enemies—within yourself. And those enemies which we speak of so often are the tendencies of the mind and body to reach out for diversions and excitements and indulgences. As I have said before, many of these things in themselves are not harmful. It is how you value them that makes them enemies—or not. Fast and pray, as he said, to keep the ground you have won a holy place; and by fasting and praying I mean a state of mind, an alertness, an awareness of where you are, what you are. You are either in light or darkness, up or down, depending upon the quality of your thought; this is not a duty but a glorious opportunity, this choosing what you shall be and living in spiritual action. Fasting means not drifting, not letting yourself go to shapeless thought, for desires are there and appetites. Prayer is adoration, it is surrender to the inner glory, to the gentle spirit that will lift you so that your foot shall not stumble.

I am going to ask you to read the following dialogue, for I believe you will hear your own voice in it, and that you will recognize the other voice as well.

First Voice: How easily the senses keep us in a state of fear!

Second Voice: That is because you live in them, through them, by them.

F. V.: How else?

S. V.: If you live from within, abiding in the Spirit, you would come to know and trust it and its power against the evidences of the senses. What is material, concrete to you, you believe in. Fear is faith in your antagonist.

F. V.: If I could know satiety instead of the besieging appetites of mind and body!

S. V.: No; ask for dominion, "bringing every thought into captivity." It is an inspiring freedom.

F. V.: What use to try an impossible thing?

S. V.: Do not question; it was done. An infinite love meets every effort and the reward is commensurate with divine understanding. Besides, it is really joyous!

F. V.: Can I say, "Today I will walk in the true way," with any confidence that I shall succeed at all?

S. V.: It is your safety, your protection and your delight— if you will believe it.

F. V.: Oh why is my desire so easily turned aside by the beasts?

S. V.: It isn't, ultimately. "He that ploweth should plow in hope." And remember in times of pressure "that they which minister about holy things, live of the things of the temple" and that "every man that striveth for mastery is temperate in all things."

F. V.: It is a lonely fight.

S.V.: No one is alone: He said, "he that sent me is with me, the Father hath not left me alone."

F. V.: That I might know him as my involuntary self-control!

S. V.: Ask—that your joy may be full!

∽

SOME OF YOU SAY, WHY IS THIS SILENCE YOU SPEAK OF SO important? Or, he is a mystic; as if that put a person outside of the life of practical religion. What is religion? What is a "faith"? Are they not worship of God and a belief that we can know him? Jesus said that eternal life was a state of mind, that is, if knowing something is a state of mind, when he said, "And this is life eternal, that they might *know* thee. . . ."

Let us be quite honest and ask ourselves how we can know him and if there is any other way than through communion with him as well as how that communion can be made. Can we learn anything without listening, even in the sense of scholastic study? Complete attention in a classroom is the first step in an institution of learning.

The student with a steadfast heart, whose first desire is to learn of him and worship him, must in the end give complete attention; "He that hath ears to hear, let him hear." Surely the two commandments of Jesus were given by him in their logical order; thou shalt love the Lord thy God, and thy neighbor as thyself. Can we love our neighbor as he meant us to do it without knowing anything of the love of God? Paul answers that in no uncertain terms, "Though I bestow all my goods to feed the poor . . . it profiteth me nothing. Though I have all faith so that I could remove mountains, and have not love, I am nothing."

To have eternal life through knowledge of God is to learn of him, to learn of his love from him, and then to put it into action in our everyday world. Acts without faith can work good but faith without acts is hard to imagine, and the consequences are inevitable. Neither way belongs to the children of God who desire to come into knowledge of their godhood.

How can we learn of him except through communion with him? How commune with him except in silence? It can only be through putting aside for intervals of quiet all human activities, not only of the hands but of the mind. And if you think you are master of your mind watch your mind when you try to still it.

Let us make an image that will help you. Suppose you wished with all your heart to be in his presence and suddenly Christ appeared to you to teach you. Would you have a thought of any importance whatever to offer him? Could any human experience matter in the least? Could you listen and hear unless you offered your mind completely to him? What prayer conceived in your mind would matter at all? What human act, what experience received through the senses would contribute to the transcendent experience of simply being aware of him?

And yet you say, I believe he dwells within me.

Do you clean the room of your mind and invite him in to reveal himself to you? Not that you may talk to him?

Why must we go to him in silence and not in prayer as we usually know it?

Because he said, ". . . I will not leave you comfortless, I will come to you . . . and he that loveth me shall be loved of my father and I will love him and will manifest myself to him."

If therefore ye are intent upon wisdom a lamp will not be wanting and a shepherd will not fail, and a fountain will not dry up.

Anonymous

ᔐ

LET US CONTINUE OUR TALK BEGUN IN THE LAST LETTER. How can we invite him in, he that is the eternal guest? What can we do that he may "manifest himself" to us? More than one has asked if there is not a "technique." I am tempted to wonder if such a question does not indicate the lack of simplicity that is required. But let us see what we can give in primer talk. First, I refer you to our last letter. Can the human mind bring anything but worship and a desire to know to that still place of quiet where he comes to reveal himself?

It is therefore necessary that we make a time and place for these communions. Later on you will find there is no place where you cannot turn your mind to him and find him; while walking, waiting at street corners, during a lull in conversation and through making the humblest work an act of praise. Laughter is a door that is always near! Joy and a lifted spirit are part of the eternity in which you can live with him now.

The simple instructions I give here are for the beginner; and let him always remember that "when thou shalt search for me with all thy heart, thou shalt find me." Find him and the way to him, if the desire is great enough.

Find a comfortable chair in a quiet room; if that is difficult go into one of the many churches that are always open. You will at once feel a self-consciousness, but as you have no audience that will pass. If there is tension in the body relax it, for bodily tension indicates mental tension. Put aside a quarter of an hour; a short time you may say, but in less than three minutes you will find that not only does your body want to walk away, but your mind has begun to race.

It is rather humiliating to find how little we are masters of our minds. But be very gentle and say to your body, as you would to a child, "I think you had better sit still in that chair until I tell you to go." For the racing, undisciplined mind I would suggest that at first you repeat, whenever it is necessary to call it back, some of the great words which have been given to us because the Spirit dwells in them, in the knowledge they bring to us of it. Repeat very gently and only as often as the mind slips away from you, one of these sentences. "I keep him in perfect peace whose mind is stayed on me." "I will not leave you comfortless, I will come to you." One wrote in the fourteenth century: "If thou desirest to have thy intent lapped and folden in one word so that thou mayest have better hold thereon, take thee but a little word which (may in thy case) accordeth better with the work of the spirit. And such a word is this word GOD or this word LOVE. Choose whichever thou wilt and fasten this word to thine heart." But choose what will best bring you to the infinite stillness within yourself, not forgetting that after you have become practiced you can find it wherever you are, in the noise and confusion of the street if you so wish. Do not look for anything, for there should be no sensation, no ecstasy. It should be an experience of extreme simplicity, natural and divinely normal. Your part is to "bring into captivity every thought to the obedience of Christ, casting down imaginations and every high thing that exalteth itself."

One said many centuries ago, "For at the first time when thou dost it thou findest but a darkness, thou knowest not what, saving thou *feelest in thy will a naked intent unto God.* . . . He asketh no help but only thyself. He wills thou do but look upon Him and let Him alone. . . . Love knocks and enters, all else stands without." And St. Denis prayed, "I beseech thee to draw us up to the shining height of thy inspired speakings where all secret things that are divine be covered under the sovereign-shining darkness of wisest silence."

And our Lord Jesus Christ said, "What I tell you in darkness, that speak ye in light."

If the tumult of the flesh were hushed, hushed the images of water, earth and air, hushed also the poles of heaven, yea, the very soul herself, hushed all dreams and imaginary revelations and whatsoever exists only in transition, having roused only our ears to Him who made them, and He alone speaks, not by them but by Himself that we may hear His word, not through any tongue of flesh, nor Angel's voice, nor sound of thunder, nor in the dark riddle of a similitude,—then we might hear Whom in these things we love, might hear His Very Self.

St. Augustine, *Confessions,* A.D. 353

HERE HE IS, HERE HE IS! I CANNOT SAY HERE HE STANDS, FOR that would be placing him materially. The nearest way to his nearness is through a refined essence of spirit. If you could distill thought you would get near the refinement. As thought is to emotion, so this quality of perception and feeling is to thought. That is why it is impossible for human thought to conceive it. He is here, eternally here, your friend and saviour and that is why meditation, the laying aside of human thought which is a heavy mechanism is so essential.

You know you have had glimpses into this world of spirit when you have sat on a mountain or by the sea and been awed into a stillness beyond your ordinary stillness by a sunset or a universe of stars; that silence beyond silence is the silence he presses through, and the flaming powers, the inspirations, the immortalities; this is the Presence, the pure Presence. Here is where it is all accomplished, for this is he, eternally here.

The love of Jesus Christ here is personal in so far as it broods over you, through you in this region unreachable, untouchable except through the refinement that takes place in your silences. It may be that you can touch it for only very short moments, yet that is enough to live on forever more.

Therefore your God is personal to you inasmuch as you have reached through feeling, past thought into infinite inducing silence. . . . He is here.

It is peace to you, health to your body, to your mind and heart. You will be sweetened when you quiet emotion, quiet thought and are still, to meet your heavenly comforter. So close your eyes, put away all thought and lie deep in the silent reaches where you will be restored, reborn, made new. Here he is.

*Christ shall come to thee showing thee His consola-
tion if thou make for Him within thee a worthy
dwelling place; all his glory and honour is within
and there is His plesaunce.*

Thomas a Kempis, 1379-1471

✍

IN THE LAST TALK WITH YOU THE APPROACH TO SILENT
meditation was given you. Today I am going to tell you a
little of both the peace and perplexity that one meets when
first starting upon this way. First let me say with all the emphasis I can, that difficult as it is, particularly for the beginner,
it is the easiest and happiest way and the chief problem is
getting used to the newness of it; of turning about and walking
in another direction with the old human arguments tugging
at us.

You have read the words, "Take no thought . . . seek ye
first the kingdom. . . . Trust me and I will make plain thy
path." But many of you have not acted upon them, upon
the truth hidden in them although you have given a loyal
belief; but that is not enough; you must seek and search with
all your heart and with all *your mind*, and the reason for this
is because in perfect silence you can be at one with the Father
and from such immortal silence comes serenity, confidence,
and wisdom for your life. In the beginning you may have a
change of feeling which is encouragement, but many do not
get out of that antechamber.

We are trying to make you understand that the august
stillness which comes when you are alone with your high
resolve is so beyond your ordinary comprehension that you
may think nothing has taken place, as if there were no results. It is difficult for the human mind to enter the inner

consciousness where the Spirit dwells because of the old habit of the mind to wander, to be excited by the human things that interest and compel attention. But with gentleness bring your mind back to your purpose; "Watch therefore, for you know not when your Lord cometh." For he will come, at first perhaps as delicately as a breath. Ask yourself, should you not earn it by your steadfast purpose? Why should we receive it instantly, with no renewed faith?

A cathedral in all its splendor and lofty beauty gives you satisfaction because you see it, hear it and react to its great solemnity. It has to the uninspired mind more power than going into the invisible, into the *idea cathedral* which was in the architect's mind before anything was made manifest, before thought was born from the invisible desires and conceptions and needs of man.

A strange thing, this love of God. I say I love God and go eagerly to sit in his presence and then nothing happens. My conscious mind travels down every bypath of present or past events and I am as far away from God as *my own mind*. But to comfort you I tell you that the performance of the act, the intent toward him, will bring what you need. Tiredness will be drawn away, strain lifted and though you feel as if nothing great had happened it is a little as if the captain of a ship at sea had changed his course and the passengers had not been aware that he had turned toward a new horizon on the way to safety.

Let these words lead you through the very small door that leads to timeless eternal space and beauty. "I surrender to Thy divine guidance; I bathe in Thy light. Of myself I can do nothing. All life cometh from Thee. Thou art the life of my life. Thou art before time; order my life and teach me the way to go. Give me the faith and power to fulfill Thy word for Thou art the holy Spirit, and Comforter."

W E HAVE TALKED ABOUT THE STARTLE OF DAILY LIFE, HOW it is not the reality, but the dream life that you see. For when you are plunged into the sea of sensuous existence, your true life leaves you like smoke. It evaporates into the stuff of dreams; it is hard to hold yourself to yourself. Let us try to understand the deep meaning of atonement, at-one-ment.

Your past experiences are past indeed; those strains and emotions of sensuous life are gone and what has remained is the temple of your own building, that edifice not built by hands. The reality of you is in the invisible, the intangible. In retrospect your spiritual milestones stand stronger to you in their fixed positions than any outward experience. Having arrived at this understanding try now, quietly, gently, without too much effort of self-discipline, to keep in the invisible, train yourself to keep immaterial. Watching and praying are essential. When hard pressed by old habits and you are under the heavy blanketings of times and events, you, as it were, disappear. This is the moment to step back into the invisible, for then the invisible will enfold you and give you great power in the visible world.

Acquire new habits; I cannot tell you how, I can only try to awaken your desire. If your desire is to be in the presence of the infinite omniscient Spirit it must mean that you lay down your sensuous material life that you may find strength and happiness, beauty and knowledge, by being in holy communion with the Spirit within. Do not misunderstand me in this; play is good, is necessary and normal; pleasures are important; the question is—What does your mind feed upon? What is your scale of values? To meet this Spirit within, which is invisible to the human life, you must acquire a quality and a technique in dwelling in the invisible while in the visible.

You know, you sense, as does the race in spite of its trial and error existence, that there are forces beyond our understanding. As you become stronger in your realization of this immortality within you, the clearer will the way be revealed to you . . . how to keep yourself dissolved and refined in the betraying, impinging, benumbing, outer visible world that you may find yourself strong and serene while in the flesh. See your true self as a high mountain, calm and lofty, still and eternal. The daily task, the mean, the malicious, the challenging, the seeming meaninglessness of this little, measured existence—see through them all while you are in them, to the lofty pinnacles of your inner self. Nothing here has scale; limitless, infinite, transcendent.

Now that you know, now that you begin to realize your godhood, take measures to keep invisible in a visible world, immortal in a mortal world, eternal in a changing world, continually reborn in a dying world.

He shall take holiness for an invisible shield.
                              Wisdom of Solomon

❧

IN ANSWERING YOUR AGE-OLD QUESTION I FEAR I MUST GIVE the age-old answer. What you suffer from is what everyone suffers from, the rusting, the tarnish of everyday life in the effort to keep the spirit shining; but as my brother said, I say to you—hold, do not let go. The temptation to distraction is childlike and common to all of us and is in the consciousness of the race. Nations tarnish, too, and rot and weaken and invite violence and suffering. To wash away the heavy oiliness of materialism is a task requiring the constant vigilance of the brotherhood, and this idea with its suggestion of effort sometimes tires one. For this reason I would like to give you the evidence of my own experience.

Some of us, all our lives long, think we cannot do a certain thing; suddenly we are forced to act, and behold, we do it and know a great satisfaction. Well, then, do not stay behind with your beggar thoughts and sit outside the cathedral with these rascals, who tempt you to say, "The task is too difficult. I am this, I am that, I fell here, I fell there." No, stand up and shake off these fears which will first drain and numb you then steal your garment of immortality and tear it into rags, taking the light out of it and changing its color to ashen gray. No! Don't idle with the wailers and the complainers, but march into the temple and stand among the radiant company where you belong. Take your place with the good and the immortal and the everlasting, the serene and the mighty, the merciful and the glorious. Who are these? How do you reach them? My brother, these are the saints, always waiting. Don't you see that by steadfastly holding to them you will be pulled away and up and brought before the high table with its damask, white as the highest heaven? Do not lag back in dreary contemplation, but act on the highest impulse. By saying that you are a poor, weak sinner, by naming these attitudes of unworthiness, you are so much delayed. Of course, it is a struggle: out of rock, then out of mud, then out of heavy liquid, then water, then air, then light—then more light, then thought, and here we are.

You know well that these beggars outside the temple, these temptations, have each a distinct personality, each a characteristic; is it not true? Therefore, each is a thought. The ancients said that beauty was to be found in the treasury of memory, memory of our flight with the gods; in memory and in intuition. And as you have been tempted by thought, so you can reach the divine experience by thought. Who could be a spineless worm if he turned his mental face toward that sweating face of him who once carried a cross!

Only one thing do I know that has been my gift, which has brought to my humble parish the simple and the hurt. That one thing is that I must never, never whine nor sit down with my old body and pity it. No, I learned that to think of the man of Galilee and hold him in my mind made for me a habit so that I was always looking past the people around me, waiting to catch a glimpse of his garment. And by thus thinking, when tempted to dawdle with the mourners, I found to my amazement I was an invited guest, and now behold, I am blinded by the glory about me.

What makes me wonder is the simplicity and naturalness of it. So don't stop to think with the beggars in their rags, but go searching among your thoughts and family and friends and times for the sight of his garment and you, too, will be an honored guest.

My last word is again, watch your thought; peg it high; hold it there, for you will not find this an effort, it will not be tiring, because peace can only be found in action. That is why you will find great hearts among the humble, because they work. It isn't as the poets tell, that they find comfort in the earth. No, it is in the glory of the mind.

He doth not force us, but after divers manners gives drink to those that will follow Him, that none go away disconsolate or die of thirst; for from this rich spring issue rivers, some great, others small ones, and sometimes pools for little children since that sufficeth them, and the beholding of a great water would but more affright them.

St. Teresa, 1515-1582

You are in that place to testify.

Emerson's *Journal*, 1803-1882

∽

YOU ENTERTAIN THE SPIRIT BECAUSE OF THE DESIRE WITHIN you; spasmodically, it is true, and with irregularity, but the desire is there. And the Spirit you have entertained has burned away heavy impurities—ignorance and heavy lethargies. And the burning away of dross through spiritual growth is the beginning of spiritual health. The spiritual action to let in light and more light, spirit and more spirit, with its understanding and power, is a gift that will make you free, for it will teach you to stand within your inner you and look out undismayed through the outer you. You are beginning to change the base of your operations. I will explain in simple allegory what has happened, for your help; for those, who, like yourself, have sought the way for the way's sake, go through a definite process.

It is as if, before you had self-conscious understanding, you had been encased in clay and the clay took on life and went about its business carrying the sleeping you within. Clay, being clay, took on the spirit of clay life. One day the clay of your particular entity was pierced by a light, a revelation which woke this sleeping you, and the clay-self turned to it and found a comforting remembrance, peace and reassurance. You became more alive, or better still, more awake. This is a clumsy picture of what has taken place, but it may help to show you how after more light poured through because of your awakened desire, the clay began to dry, and turn to dust and cracked and gave way, so that the outer encasement is growing thinner and thinner. This is an inward picture, it has nothing to do with the body except as the body reflects health and release. Those who are doing what you are attempting are spared much of the bludgeoning the clay is heir to. Instead of going through fire to be tempered you deliberately ignite and illumine yourself with this inward flame. You burn yourself free and step clear of the rough and tumble, the trial by error and the hard law of consequences that wait in the dark for those who carry no lamps. In this there is great responsibility and great joy.

If the weaknesses are not met spiritually, they thicken the clay again and faith becomes dulled, tarnished. Do you not begin to realize the importance of the working method of examining the moment as it comes and making it spiritual? You have sensed at last that when an outside problem of vexation or decision comes, instead of letting your outer you be consumed, it is happier to keep in your divine personality.

Burn your own dross, temper your own steel, and be spared. Not through a selfish motive nor through fear of punishment, but through love of truth and beauty. Goodness and mercy, order and beauty and inspiration are in this inner you, and this heavenly radiance is melting away the dross of old habits, mental states, weaknesses, inertias and fears; not only those of your lifetime but those inherited through the past from the race. It is a large order that you have asked for! Therefore keep released from tensions, relax in quiet and in the confidence which is your strength.

ᔆ

IT IS AS IF YOU CLIMBED AND REACHED A PLATEAU WHERE you could rest and consolidate your gains for awhile and gather strength through an inner, eternal voice. You go on and up with so much less dross until you reach another plateau and lie a little weary, but with a most wondrous sense that you are stronger; so you go, ever climbing and getting freer from delaying emotions and habits. That is being shriven. So in this clay, and workaday, violent life, march gaily upward out of the teeming plains, through the dark forests, up on to the cliffs where the way is less crowded. Climb the heights and soon you will find you have escaped and are alone in the clear air, air that is revivifying, restoring. Be a good athlete, self-disciplined, tried and free. It may seem strange to give you a picture where there is so much effort and struggle—for it is not so; the yoke is easy, the burden is light compared to the way of the flesh. There is no effort spiritually, though you find you have to do things that tire the body, for you carry with you your knowledge of high peace like a lofty mountain peak high up in the silence near the stars. As one has said, "What I say is commonplace, but if it became a conviction it would change the faith of the world."

> *Nor stoney tower, nor walls of beaten brass,*
> *Nor airless dungeon, nor strong linkes of iron,*
> *Can be retentive to the strength of Spirit . . . .*
>
> Shakespeare, *Julius Caesar*

∽

LET US CONSIDER THE INSTRUCTION "TAKE NO THOUGHT OF what ye shall say" or do. Take no thought. There is a tendency to become self-conscious in spiritual striving, there is an itch to do good, a sense of an effort to help. There are many spiritual busybodies! But the gift a man has with animals, or with children and flowers is inarticulate and silent and unself-conscious, without words that have been thought out. It is because no one has any idea of what is felt by those around him if he is one-pointed to the Source within.

As we have said so often, your whole task is to take steps that lead to that secret place and when the last step is taken and you sit in silence with the Word you become one with the Spirit, with the power back of all manifested life, infinitely gentle when you give yourself to it. That is where all things are done for you, where the crooked ways are made straight, where doors are opened and influences pass through to others without your knowing it. When you do this you carry a hidden virtue that you cannot measure nor even sense. Be careful about wasting time in what you call helping, for that can be dangerous. No, you lose what you have when you think you have a power, you lose it when you think you are an influence. If it is your good fortune to be an instrument so great and dynamic, you must, perforce, renounce all personal gratification in what materialists call "your inspiration" to others. All must be stern and strong and clean and free from the false valuations of sentimentality. Take the steps to your inner self with the naked intent to worship him in his holiness and all will be set in motion with beauty and order. That is all you can do and what you are needed to do. In this way the doors open to let in light and you, too, are released when you are still and open your heart so that the Father can do the work.

To a racked and unhappy soul the offer of such peace and immortal gladness seems a mockery, and yet that is the eternal challenge. It is also rebirth if the way is accepted, the birth of the Christ within. Every one of us has to find the humble stable, the lowly place of the dumb animals, and under our own bright star find the Christ and the gift of everlasting faith.

We who are facing a world of unleashed savagery must for our life's sake plunge into the immortal living Presence, melt into that healing freedom from the world, that lies within. There, guarded by courage and humility, is the Christ, and going to that place of holiness and light is all that is asked of you.

When you reach this deep subjective realm through your desire, whether it be through physical love or the desire for spiritual attainment, it is in obedience to the same law. When physical love leaves the self-conscious state then the deep subjective knowledge and wisdom take charge and new life is born. The spiritual desire for attainment goes through the same steps but the desire is stronger, for inherent in that desire is a knowledge of eternal life, and though it is quiet in its manifestations during the self-conscious period, once past the threshold, the deep subjective realm receives your idea, your desire, your prayer and it is given life and reality in due course. The birth through physical love is but a primitive conception compared to the rebirth through thought and aspiration and prayer. The same process takes place but is a thousand times more swift than the first.

If, therefore, human love and birth are solemn, vital, mysterious, how much more so is the birth of thought, a creative idea. Consider how an idea is conceived . . . through desire always; and that desire is aroused by many things; pain, rebellion, suffering. Once the idea is truly conceived the involuntary processes take charge and the rebirth is instant.

So be aware of the vitality of your thought, and it is vital, because it is the sum total of your character. When you rise and break through the mesh of ignorance the light of understanding clears the atmosphere around you and you see the star. The air is crystal and you behold the Child.

In this high purity because of a new sensitiveness, you will understand that your thoughts, your ideas, your resistance, your acceptances are organic, vital, and will always obey the law of conception and birth. You will realize that when you make a stand and say, "This is what I will think," you are reborn.

"The Word was made flesh, the Word was made flesh!"

Take the thought that leads you to the secret place of the

Most High, but when you reach that place you can do nothing but worship, nothing but give yourself and all you desire to Infinite Love.

As never before let all who serve him at this time prepare the place for the birth of his Son, for the sake of the world, for the sake of those who sit in darkness. Adorn and praise and sing his glory for his light is everlasting and giveth peace.

Then when all things were wrapped in deepest silence, to me was uttered the hidden Word.

This must you know also, that the soul hath inward freedom, and she cometh forth without help and without images, that God may freely unite Himself with her.

Meister Eckhart, 1260-1327

BE LIKE A CHILD; LOOK AT THY TWO FEET AND SAY, LORD, walk these for me. Talk to him as to thy friend and nurse. Be in sweet common friendship with him. Call him in thy bath, in thy daily tasks, in thy going from one room to another. Say, Nay, I will not go alone. Come, be thou with me, lead thou the way. Behold, he will answer then, and come running like laughter and golden hope into thy heart, and with understanding love will he walk with thee from room to room. And, too, will he stand beside thee when thou faceth thy friends and visitors, and he will place a hand in thine and will watch thy heart and the issues therefrom so that thou canst talk in perfect safety knowing that thy words will be food and drink and life to all in thy presence.

For thou hast him all to thyself. He is thine—forever. Do not puzzle how he can see thy two feet when there are millions of feet, that is too much for thine understanding. Enough that it is the truth that he hath never failed to come when

called and that he will come as thou dost want him. He is
to be sought through the refinements of the heart. Go, then,
and ask him to rest thee, to heal thy complaints, and to fill
thee with the strong virtue required. He will manifest, he
never faileth. He is thy Saviour and sweet comforter. So go
into thy immediate and personal life with him for thy very
own, with thy hand in his. Let him smooth thy pillow, smooth
thy blanket; and in deep, loosened sleep let him teach thee
that the Life immortal, perfect divine Sonship with him, can
be known in all its fullness by such a simple way as this childlike invitation to him—the eternal Guest.

> *Be able to be alone. Lose not the advantage of soli-*
> *tude . . . but delight to be alone and single with*
> *Omnipresency. . . . Life is a pure flame, and we live*
> *by an invisible sun within us.*
>
> Sir Thomas Browne, 1605-1682

THERE IS A DIVINE ILLUMINATION FROM EARTHLY THINGS
that will bring great joy and heavenly release to you if
seen through the pure eyes of the Spirit; when you bathe,
when you eat, when you walk, when you sleep—these are
great symbols and are holy. When you work changing the unseen into maintenance (which you do when you use your
mind to earn your bread) be holy by pouring the light upon
humble ordinary things, for thus will you be transfigured
and your day be blessed to you. Also it is one way to overcome
the world which can be made a constant sacrament. Have
more joy in your daily life, for renouncing the world is first
of all to have a greater zest for things infinite than things
finite. The idea of renouncing joy is destructive; have greater
joy, but be sure the source of it is within rather than with-

out—and, lest you be misled, that simply means to be more aware of him you worship while you play, for he abides in a lifted heart. He overcame the world; put the world, therefore, at his feet. Sometimes in the past you have gone across the no-man's-land we have talked about for inspiration and then you have left it behind you and have stood in your workaday world and expected to get results for your workaday spirit. No! Results may come that way, but slowly, inadequately. Your direct action is when you go back to your world charged and supercharged and stay charged. I have spoken at length on this for it is time you were more awake to your own power within. Go, therefore, plunge, experiment, do it gaily; nothing is too simple, too tiny. Go and move mountains and awake! The outward thrust of faith is your stand.

∽

HOLD THE PEARL OF GREAT PRICE, HOLD THE TALISMAN— believing. The secret lies in the reality of the power of this shining faith. Rest on it as you would on the arm of a strong friend, realizing its actuality. As fear attracts evil events so doth faith attract good events. An act of faith is no idle thing, it is the first step.

Dissolve everything to a fiery thought, a thought of fiery faith. When fears of defeat come, burn them up so that not for an instant can they take hold. You can do everything by being there first.

Do not waste too much thought looking into yourselves wondering what you ought to do; keep a "naked intent" toward God, keep one-pointed in your advance into the seeming chaos and darkness of the world. It makes for the capacity of loving stillness, it makes the temple of the bosom hold the spirit more adequately, it makes for gentle holiness, comfort and protection, stillness and softness, that you may stand strong and alert. Those to whom this is revealed are the lonely, but like the mountaintop, lonely in the clouds; the air is pure.

Be patient, be patient, don't fret—leave that to the little. Do not be afraid of standing to your full measurement, that inward measurement you know so well. And yet do not try to be perfect; that is a paradox, but too much effort is a delayer. Be gentle with yourself, you cannot storm the kingdom, for those who feel the weight are heavy burdened . . . that is the first stage.

And yet again be soft with everyone but yourself; it is a fine tonic, good iron for the blood. This is but a hint—a little bit of good salt for the sauce.

At this time when events come thick and fast do not linger emotionally on sights and sounds and rumors. Accept them as facts and leave them. Even in battle when our best friends fell beside us, we saluted and passed on. So it is with you in this great battle; do what you can but remember that your constant fight is to keep your holy stillness high above the din. Hold it—and however much there is thunder and darkness and you are appalled by multiplying dangers, even if they advance in terrifying hosts, hold and advance! Then this stillness, illumined, will come into your lives on this earth and great peace and goodness and glory and beauty will be your adventure. It is right that you attack, always advance keeping your fighting edge outside you. But from within fill your bosom with light and high inspiration, for then is the kingdom of heaven brought down into your material world. It takes courage; therefore take courage and give it!

> *The things we cherish most are at the mercy of the things we cherish least.*
>
> William James, 1842-1910

Love, and do what you like.

St. Augustine

⟳

WE ALL KNOW THAT THE HUMAN YOU IS CONTRARY, IT IS the way the animal is made, for man is always contrary to his inner self and the problem is to melt these two into one so that there is no conflict. There may be help in taking a sort of lazy lying-in-the-sun attitude when caring too much about people, material things, injustice and meanness.

When tempted to emotional upheaval say, "Hold; this is too good to waste on little things, I will put it into vigor or discipline." So many tired people are enraged by the little things of life and use heavy artillery when a word would do. Great forces are in you, do not let them loose in any other way at this time, than to make them build your holy temple. Remember how you were told of the delicacy of thought; when you harden in human irritation you use too much power on unimportant things. Therefore keep yourself in practice on little things, for that steaming and straining over stupidities is not worth the emotion spent on them. Save this mighty power to keep yourself where your life will be renewed, balanced, rested and fortified.

It is difficult not to be subject to the enraging fires of personalities, but personalities are only states. You will find some arid, some boiling, some terrifying, some evil and when you meet or even talk of one you can turn on a destructive force which, though you soon forget it, is very tiring in result. It is so easy to be put off your guard; watch others and notice how the appetite for anger and critical resentment poisons their thoughts.

What I am trying to tell you is that the beauty you seek is

so easy to find but is only found by being always on guard, not being tempted off it an instant. No; smile and walk with easy confidence among all sorts of states of consciousness and be so illumined from within that they too will become purified. These contacts cannot stain nor tire nor block you. Oh, my dear child, it is such a wonderful way to find rest! Practice on little things and little people and you will see how immediate will be your release—your release from what is called "the weary world." Laugh and shine on them impersonally and you will see the coming of a light so clear it will be as if until then you had only peered through foggy mists.

Be secretly aware and restfully industrious in keeping your thoughts in that place where the air is as bright as fine glass or pools in marble basins—where beauty is transcendent. It is a place where there is no longing; that is the tenderness mixed in the amazement, for here hope is fulfilled. Stay then in this stillness so heavenly that the poets can only reach it in high lonely moments. Keep in this place, for the tender and the great moments which have lifted you far above dull realities are all here; honor and bright hopes are here, true courage is here. Do not be fearful ever of being fearful, but rather abide where you will be given those things that will protect you.

The way, then, is to still the conflict between your inner and outer selves, to join hands and present yourself before him, that you may rise to your true stature in his presence; here all strain and effort and contrariness will pass away like running shadows. Do not worry and allow your thoughts to swell into heavy mountains but keep in this place and let the details of your life resolve. Not to fret over nonessentials when one can breathe a cool strong air, is what is meant.

And remember, never knit your brow, keep it holy!

For crooked thoughts separate from God.

Wisdom of Solomon

IT MAY SEEM STRANGE TO YOU THAT YOU MUST BE WEAK TO be strong, that you gather the power invincible from the small elusive secret fountain within, which can only be found through thought. It is elusive because though it is there, eternal, it does not press; it must be sought; and there are so many things that delay the seeker. It is indeed a pilgrim's progress. But be of good cheer, much has already fallen away from you that is dross and you feel a certain freedom from fear and you sense your divine protection. Accept your responsibilities gaily, happily. Take these disciplines that you set up for yourselves like a happy game, for it can be most joyful. Soon you will discover that when you are in it—this game—you are all right and when you are out of it you are all wrong. Therefore employ every method you can to be near the fountain and the reward will be your deeper enjoyment of life. That is the testimony that has come down from the saints.

If you examine history and the lives of those you admire you will find they all held to an unseen confidence; something, as they would say, came out of the depths to their rescue when everything was against them and they were challenged by despair, defeat and delay. You cannot judge anything on the outside nor analyze the struggle while you are in it. Out of the past has come great wisdom for those who can hear— and everyone now is challenged by iron events. You may ask, "How can we deal with the situation if we cannot understand it from the outside or analyze it when it is here?" Largely by feeling. You cannot analyze a feeling of faith when all is against a leader, that spark that turned the tides of men; that unshakable serenity of one who calm yet vigilant, held to the unseen, heard the voice of the Comforter and found inward strength. That is all we can do for you—give you friendly assurances of its reality—"yea though I walk through the valley of the shadow": that is the essence of all we can be to you. But do not be dismayed, you are safe as long as you hold. A great fire is burning. See that there is no dross about you and you will come through unscathed. Life has always been dangerous and no one is spared the conflict within himself, though a joyful courage attracts a joyful life.

The defense of your inward realm must be taken by guardian thoughts, the guardian thoughts that will surround your inner source; then you will not need to worry so much about the outward details; meet them as they come, inspirationally. Lift your spirits high and be undismayed by the scenery! You cannot add one cubit to your inspiration, but you can protect it. Bend every energy of mind to that purpose, lift it high, make a gallant surrender of your whole existence to lifting the light of your inspiration into every act, into your bodies, into your minds. Be illumined through and through. Consider yourself a magnifying glass through which all your thoughts and experiences are one-pointed, and your inspiration from within will concentrate into a burning point. That is being strong. *Such august faith restores the instant.* You are a son of God—go forth! It is true that your outer you sits down like Peter and weeps and denies. It is true that your crown becomes heavy and your shield of great weight and the sword slips your hand from too much dwelling in the world, which is ignorant and fearful and darkening and ready to steal your garment of immortality. No! Concentrate on your inward light and to such magnitude will it grow that the crown will rest lightly, the shield will take a lifting of its own and the sword will shine in your hand.

This is the burning up of dross—turning every impulse to this heroic stand.

THESE ARE IRON TIMES FOR THE NATIONS. BE ALL THE MORE disciplined in your emotions, for you will hear cries of fear and the cowards will try to force you into their quaking cul-de-sacs. No, be ready for their poison and their unpreparedness. It is the time to hammer out the metal of your shining armor. Remember you are of the rank of the shock troops, without fear, dismay or self-indulgence. Watch, then, all appetites and ponder them carefully This is important; nothing is too small, too subtle, too tiny. When big events are cutting the air like scimitars it is well not to have indulgence; see and watch with vigilance the little enemies.

Again as an old soldier, I say, attack without effort the idea of happiness. Insist on it, demand it, fill your body with happiness like good strong wine, for from the beauty of a lifted heart come the joyful issues of life. Now is the time to rise up and tambour your spirit with drumsticks of joy! So will you drum yourselves free that you may go down before unbelief. Unbeliefs are of your own making; that is hard to grasp but the time will come when we can look back together and laugh. The way to freedom is to have freedom in the thoughts of your head, and at this hour when all about are most materially inclined it is good to be aware.

As for this idea of happiness do not misunderstand me; it is the joy of courage which brings the faith to win. Let in the rays and beams to every situation, for such is the kingdom of light. March bravely with the brave, demand this joy, this morale, for with immortality on your banners, and happiness in your trumpets, you will march on together into such a brightness it is as if the sun came down to join you on your road.

> *In the deserts of the heart*
> *Let the healing fountain start*[1] . . .
>   W. H. Auden, 1907——

∽

I HAVE MUCH SYMPATHY FOR YOU FOR I KNOW WHAT IT IS
when it seems as if you were wrapped in heavy blankets
so that you cannot move—the blankets of inertia, of cold fear
and apprehension; blankets of melancholy. And when you
make the effort to throw them off for an intake of spiritual inspiration they are suddenly tighter than ever, so tight that
the mind is also blanketed.

In times like these one is lifted up to high resolution and
then dropped back to irresolution and uncertainty. Pinpricks
of events, personalities pressing in from all sides are magnified. Indeed it is hard to remember your Creator in your
human life! So often it is said that it is important to face
realities; but it is hard to know what is real and what is beyond real . . . one cannot see the forest for the trees. We can
only repeat what we have said before; your only reality is
your inward at-one-ment with the Spirit within you. You
touch it, you lose it to find it again, to forget it. And yet your
desire for the companionship of the Spirit has grown so that
you are aware of the protection and bounty of the Almighty
and that you are guided and given strength again to meet the
challenges which seem so stupid and unfair.

Human life is beset with challenges; it is true of any form
of discipline. You will always be in conflict with the material
world; you are always bringing order out of chaos all through
your day. As we have told you before, your will to win is an

---

[1] From *Collected Poems* by W. H. Auden (New York: Random House,
Inc., 1945). Used with permission.

important part of your spiritual armor, for it goes with faith always. Through practice you are gaining more skill to play the game within—without. The without is easier because you see the play. Within is more difficult because your lacks, such as moral weaknesses, inertias, are not revealed and are often unrecognized when you see them, as it were, dramatized in ultimate action on the outside.

You know that this way of life, these communions calling for spiritual aid, is the only reality, and as you push away the heavy blankets of indifference, of old habits and weaknesses, you will find refreshment in your freedom. You will become more sensitive to instructions and you will obey them. We know that the still small voice is there to be heard and we know that every excuse is made not to find the time to listen to it. Remember in your hours of living in the world that your salvation is in the impulse to obey, the faithfulness of response to the delicate instruction. In this lies character and surely the beginning and end of our collaboration is the development of character.

Step back into this holy, immaterial, deathless timeless quietness. At times it is unbelievable that there is a serenity guiding you, healing and sustaining, and yet this is the only way to free yourselves. Say, "I will first seek the kingdom within me"; then you *can* be still, you *can* be serene, you *can* carry a cloudless sky into a frantic emotional day full of upsetting events through this obedience to the counsel you hear which comes in the sense of awareness, of peace and knowledge that your Redeemer liveth and is with you. Through him you can be a conqueror and work miracles. Work them!

> *Through want of strength I have gone to the wrong shore. Thirst came upon thy worshipper, though he stood in the midst of the waters; have mercy!*
>
> *Vedic Prayer*

DO YOU NOT SEE THAT YOU HAVE COME TO THE PLACE WHERE it is wise to practice all the time bringing the Spirit into the roughage of daily life? Can you understand it better if you say to yourselves, "By doing this I am overcoming the world"? That is, your world.

Necessity sometimes brings you to your feet; do not wait for necessity, be there first. Say, "I know that you will give me my daily bread, I know that you will guide me in the way of wisdom, I know that you will release me from the terror by night" . . . the pressure of material existence.

Do you ask, "Why am I chosen for this release?" You are not chosen, you chose and called; called to yourselves this freedom from the laws of negative consequences by abiding in the cause, the source, the Holy Spirit. You can demonstrate a working principle. To be sure you have failed, blundered, daydreamed and got lost in thickets and sloughs of despond and forgetfulness like anyone else, but you have a peculiar and individual instinct for beauty, the beauty of spiritual things, and you have sensed that you can walk into the dawning of a new day. Eternal love walks with anyone intent upon this adventure and the daily miracle comes when you can hold what you receive and do not permit it to become dissipated by your senses and the talks and alarms of self-conscious life. Go forth then, and overcome your own immediate world.

Sometimes you are bewildered for there seems so much to be done and you cannot see the forest for the trees; it is difficult, for your minds are not yet trained to realization, realization in the sense of involuntary awareness of the constant Presence. For that reason what is asked of you seems difficult to the material mind; it is not that you should make a cowardly escape from realities, it is that you should fill yourselves with a calmness not your own making, *that you become a channel* for it to flow through.

When you examine your inner human selves you find they are tornadoes, volcanoes of feeling ready without warning to ravage the world around you. With the growing consciousness of the Spirit that feeling will be transmuted, for it must be renounced, changed. This sounds as if you had to go through a sort of exercise, but reread about bringing the well-filled water jars across no-man's-land from the well of life and you will see it is not quite that. The world is too much with you. You would have more power over it if you could perceive that the shock of the world with its vital interest and absorbing drama makes the mind race and the emotions tense. Those who desire to overcome it must step back and let the mind be washed clean and the emotions put in order. This to some may sound an impossible task, but is infinitely easier than suffering the consequences of the human way.

One of you said, "I am tired of being brave!" Say it no more, for that is the negation of all that has been revealed to you. Courage enfolds you with wings, it is calm and protecting; it lifts you over rough places and is the victory of the spirit over the material world.

Another has said, "There is a human limit to what a body can do!" Of course that is so, but you can find great help sometimes by realizing your own inner strength. In the midst of fatigue and exhaustion many have been lifted to their feet by the clearness of their thought. Much of sickness is psychic and is the heaviness of materialism.

You say you are rebellious because you cannot do more. You asked how nature could show you. Consider the delicacy of the beginnings of things and how they must be nurtured; it is the same with your revelation and the way it must be nurtured. You plant a seed as you were prompted to do, for concepts and thoughts are seeds and grow much faster than nature. The weed-thoughts wither into dust instantly when you seek the quiet communions of your inner stillness; they are in the soil of illusion and have no power when you are free.

Be not troubled too much by the hobgoblins of the imagination, that is a useless burden. The reality is enough to bear without adding the unreality. The blanking out, the forgetfulness after renewal, is what must be avoided; and yet it is not a question of duty; you must not blame yourselves for it is hard for the human mind and character not to stew in its own juice! Human nature is stubborn, lazy, somnolent. Step forth into the brightness of spiritual vigor! Believe steadily, the long belief; look danger in the face and do not quail. Many ask that God come down to guide you—do your part, stand up, go up, realize your majesty; and in the deep security of your silence, realize the godhood that is yours when you are one with the Father.

There is no wall like an idea.

Emerson's *Journal*

IN OUR SEARCHING FOR THE WAY SOMETIMES ONE MOOD IS more helpful than another, and here is a very childlike one for tired spirits.

As a child when you were pushed ahead by your nurse or your mother, you had a spacious open faith; a knowledge that you were being safely guided through the unknown. Try today to recapture a feeling only half remembered deep within your place of memory, and in your imagination lie back in confidence and face the future with an open heart, knowing that the Presence who is guiding you is good, loving, protecting.

When the moment for action comes there will, of course, be much for you to do; but because of these moments of rest you will hear better when you are told what to do and how to do it.

Give out love; give royally of it, but keep silent. Build a thick area about yourself of a shock-absorbing substance, make an image of protection that will neutralize the natural alarms that you may be called upon to experience. This is first aid. Laugh and be merry for that is healing to those about you who despair. Be humble and human and tender; be selfless and patient with the forgiveness that permits you to go up to the altar; be simple. In fact be the child pushed ahead, having the knowledge that you are in safekeeping, in loving hands.

If you can live like this in the midst of everyday confusion, then you have nothing to fear. Fast and pray; keep in this core of light within your within-ness and you will be free from dread and ache and fear. Fast in thy mind; pray by accepting the joy of God and keep within where he abides. Go thy way, blest, being wheeled before the Holy Company!

～

TODAY LET US WRITE DOWN THIS PRAYER: "O HOLY SPIRIT within me, hold me in thy gentleness which gives me strength. Keep me from the strain that takes me far from thee, keep me in thy radiant presence. Keep me awake that the sleep of forgetfulness may not shut thee from me; remind me of my immortality now. I know that I am in thy love; keep me illumined and untarnished. Teach me to play my part."

In times like these we cannot go out into the world without the armor of God and the only way we can wear it is to keep our minds clothed in the idea of him all the day long. Let the Spirit within do the thinking, the talking, the listening. Stand back and let it guide your feet; you are never alone and the light within can be a comfort in the darkness to others. No word need be spoken and sometimes, perhaps many times, we feel only confusion and the limitations of our own personalities to such an extent that we doubt the reality of the power within; but if the "naked intent" is there, its light is felt without any effort on our part and sometimes without the conscious awareness of others. "Of myself I can do nothing," the Father dwelling within lives and works in me if I tether my mind to him even ever so little. And today everyone has a great obligation to keep aware faithful to the creative Power.

And here is a prayer for emergency when alarms strike with the force of a blow and you are tempted to put faith in your antagonist:

"I am on duty; thy hand I feel upon my shoulder. Let thy peace flow through my heart to all about me. I know thou livest and though I cannot see the working of the divine plan I know that my being on duty is part of the resurrection and the awakening that is to come. Here I am, aware of thy presence, thy love, thy goodness. I know I have immortality now, in this life, that thou hast placed the shield of faith upon my arm, the sword of the Spirit in my hand, the spurs of resolution and action upon my feet. I therefore dedicate myself in this hour of seeming despair, to faith, to joy and to the knowledge that I am alive in thee. I will resolve not to quail, nor to dwell in idle forboding. I dedicate myself to holding the portals of my heart wide open that I may be a channel for thy spirit. I dedicate every living hour to this resolve, to thy service. I trust in thee; I am on duty."

Some exercise themselves in many commendable practices and perform many acts of virtue. . . . This is well enough for beginners, but it belongs to a far higher perfection to follow the interior attraction of the Holy Spirit and be guided by His direction.

Louis Lallement, 1587-1635

> *Religion is not a melancholy, the spirit of God is not*
> *a dampe!*
>
> John Donne, 1573-1631

∽

AFTER REALIZING THE CONSEQUENCES OF INVOLUNTARY *un*-self-control you will perhaps know better the meaning of voluntary self-control. We all know how thoughts seize and shake us, involuntarily stealing in through the cracks in our armor, and that is why it is so important to have your inward area filled with light so that fearful thoughts cannot bear the sight and cannot find lodging space. When you are weak and the walls of your fortress are of paper upon which memory has morbidly written the mistakes of the past, how easily are they torn so that false alarms sweep through to your vitals! And how they call in the whole ghoulish family to live upon your fears. It is man's task to keep his inward self clean and luminous, radiant and aware. As eternal vigilance is the price of liberty how much more is the price of spiritual victory; how important is living day by day, hour by hour, moment by moment.

Great power will be given only where great power is generated.

When you live with the great forces that beat your heart, and work through the involuntary activities of the body, you are given assurance because of your rejection of weakening terrors, and you find immediate response in health and wisdom in your daily life. More and more will you realize the relief throughout your nervous system, and the organization of your body will collaborate and assist you in generating the spirit of victory, of "dominion over all your earth-consciousness." It is true that only the brave deserve the fair; *only the aware deserve the Spirit.*

As you desire to live spiritually, to be safeguarded, given health, simple goodness, peace of mind, and knowledge to deal with the circumstances of your life, you must come to this conclusion—I will discipline myself.

If you were asked to help a youth on his way you would guard him with constant watchfulness. Look upon yourself and see how much watching you need. Humans are so constituted that even while they are professing an intent toward a spiritual way of life they are delayed by moods, negative emotions of criticism, prejudice and self-justification as well as the daily assaults upon the mind by gossip, letters, and all the stinging gnats of daily contacts. It seems as if they were constantly setting up ninepins which are not allowed to stand in peace; the ninepins of ordered thinking are knocked over while they are being set up.

From a practical point of view it seems a difficult thing for man to do, this being continually aware of something almost unknown within himself, for man needs something to play with and it is easier for him to love a dog, a child, a woman, than the Light within which he cannot see. He is asked to love a thing imagined, at first, until it becomes the greatest reality, and that is a task indeed.

I cannot show you God, nor yourself in your illumined state. But you will grow to feel him and to turn within for healing comfort. Spiritual things can only be spiritually discerned. Desperate need and your imagination tell you why, so that you instinctively seek until the feeling, the answer comes. Through this invisible feeling-nature you are given a change of heart, and you can be assured that because of your love for what you have experienced in these moments of oneness with him, your imagination and reason will tell you that this came from an inner you, an inner light, an inner love—an inner Love!

Through love and remembrance of him, as you live minute

by minute, turn your eye inward when there is a pause, whenever you are at a street corner waiting to cross, when you
bathe; when you clothe your body, wash away the grimy
thoughts, brush away the unspoken ignorance. During your
morning preparations do not let your mind rattle with the
thoughts of the day ahead. Clothe yourself so that you will
contain, within, this love that supplies the Light, and when
there is a pause in your work, when a clock strikes the hour,
say these words: "I stand in Light. No foolish thoughts, no
foreboding, no false imagery, no terror can come near this
Light within me, for I love it and serve it and I stand here
purified, dedicated to honor, to health of mind and body, to
peace of mind and life everlasting."

This, my children, is a prescription needed in these times of
chaotic thinking, and you will find if you obey this spiritual
desire you will be led in the paths of righteousness for his
name's sake, and you will know the joy of involuntary self-control. During your times of quiet, those lovely moments, pools
of restoration where you drink deep of the waters of spiritual
health, learn to discipline yourselves. Not with the fist, for
that soon tires; not with the mind, for that is forgetful; but
with the heart. Love will keep you there. Love is vigilant, it
is quieting, it is your gently strong awareness, it is the oil of
joy that supplies the Light.

Do this in remembrance of him, for he is the Light within.

*Put all sadness from thee, for it is the sister of doubt
and anger. It is the most mischievous of all spirits and
the worst to the servants of God. Learn now, O un-
wise man! how it troubleth the Holy Spirit; remove therefore, sadness from thyself and afflict not
the Holy Spirit which dwelleth within thee.*

The Shepherd of Hermas, A.D. 142-157

LET us use imagery. Once there was a white bird with a blue bill and orange feet; it was neatly plumed and took joy in flying over waves. This bird was of the sea and lived in the far north certain seasons, and in flight took long journeys across continents to the cold again. When buffeted by winds it followed its unerring instinct, rose high, straightened its wings and held to its course in safety, clear of all danger. It flew above contrary air currents, high and over great violences, held and protected by the instinct inherent within it.

So it is with the soul that is controlled by the self-conscious realization of its relation to the power of the Spirit in which it abides.

The symbol of the bird suspended in horizontal flight, high above the tumults, the challenging fears and unreasonable panics, applies to times like these. Dark thoughts try to reach up and drag the bird from the sky, for it is the constant conflict between the outer and inner you. You have surely arrived at the place where you can in wisdom know that there is a balance that can be kept, a high air of safety that you can seek where you are protected from the wastage of false alarms that gather to form a cloud. Spread your wings to the upcurrent and rise high above, serene and confident in that power which holds you in that high altitude; fly over in a sky free from all danger, in the safekeeping of your true direction, of the knowledge of it, the instinct for it, in the desire for the manifestation in your life of the love of God.

Be the winged Word and fear nothing! Then will you be in the very center of the concept, divine instinct made manifest, which is revealed in light, in swift action, in order and balance, in protection and beauty.

You have the choice of this clear high impersonal yet loving peace, or the storms of human existence. Spread your wings straight and catch the first morning breeze of divine promise and hope, and be lifted into that high place where freed from the clutching of circumstance you can with a great heart give strength and surcease to those you love, to the world; for you have asked to be humble messengers of the Lord Jesus. In obedience to his commands your protection lies.

As a humble child, fearful and weary, do not sit down in dismay upon the unsure ground of apprehension, but take your spirit and spread it forth like the wings of the bird and let it rise high and clear into the shining sun of faith; let your spirit take wing and of a surety it will carry strength and hope into the farthest reaches of your human life.

Fly high, for thus it is that one rises from dead thoughts into immortality.

> *Somewhere within our life is a standard as invisible as the equator, as relentless as the seasons.*
>
> P. H. Elliot

⟲

IN THESE TIMES YOU CANNOT AFFORD TO MEET THE SHOCK OF life with emotion; you cannot hate, you cannot fear. The evil that you see has always been here; the ignorance is not for you to judge nor can you respond to it even in the sense of so-called righteous indignation. We have tried to teach you that you must defend yourselves with the knowledge you have received from this way of life so that you will not be dragged down into an emotional maelstrom of dark imaginings. True creative sympathy does not throw one into the darkness of another's life. Stand in the light that has been revealed to you by your communion with him who said, "My joy I give unto thee," and by so doing help to illumine the one in need. Divine wisdom is the antithesis of violence and despair; therefore if you have tendencies, like appetites, to strain and boil, to daydream, to *think black* in deep negations, you but add to the ignorance and are enslaved by it. What holds the race back but fear thoughts, greed thoughts, self-thoughts, which are of the race? . . . this strange subtle pride of race! They take so many shapes; that is why one must be forever vigilant, forever remembering, forever holding oneself to the center and letting the indwelling Spirit take possession that it may fill your life to the uttermost with the realization that this infinite presence of the Spirit is actually present, is the actual stuff of love and peace and power. And when you find yourselves pressed hard say, "I will not take in, I will give out; I will not in darkness dwell, light shall be my life. It will cleanse me and I shall go forth forgiving all things, knowing that this love will resolve all things and my way will be made straight, and I shall knock and it shall be opened unto me, and I shall find and receive."

Keep awake in the victory of the Spirit; pour out thanksgiving before there is a sign of victory; thank the Father for the event before it happens; cleanse your hearts of all prejudices and the impotent rage against nations and nationalities and all the hot emotions that boil in the hell of personality.

Keep rather in that secret place where emotion is transmuted and the human spirit is lifted by the swift transmutation. A time will come when by your steadfast voluntary discipline of the pressures of actualities and the realities of your outer world you will be aware of the involuntary transmutation which comes quietly as a reward for your intent and desire . . . your desire above all others to know him in your everyday world, to know eternal life now.

Fight on brave ones, and cast off the heavy vestments with despair in their folds! Put on the garments of immortality;

be worthy, keep yourselves shriven, be stern with no one but yourselves, and do not go this way from a sense of duty, but for the fulfillment of Joy!

> *An interior man will make more impressions on hearts by a single word animated by the spirit of God, than another by a whole discourse which has cost him much labor and in which he has exhausted all his power of reasoning.*
>
> Louis Lallement, 1587-1635

HOLD, HOLD AS YOU HAVE NEVER DONE BEFORE. WATCH EACH word and mood, beware of scattering and spilling; do anything—fall flat on the floor and wait till your valiant soul lifts you to your feet. Be ashamed of quailing. No, no! It is easy to see this great fear gripping and squeezing men into dwarfs, but, oh, my children, do not get caught in the feeling of the sick. Now is the appointed time. Hold. Do things to remind you to stay where you belong, tie knots on your fingers, put things up, hang them about so that you may train your foolish heads to remember your Creator now, and so give life to your world. I tell you in no uncertain words that what you actually think now holds your world together. One wrong evil thought coming into your galaxies (of thoughts) could sweep everything you see into Timbuctoo. Your only safety is to be within the center of your kingdom, living from within out, not from without in. Be there all the time, no compromise. You will find that it is glorious fun, and easier to be men than fearful pygmies in dark jungles, chased by wild animals—slaves to nature.

There are armies wedged behind you; lead them! They will strengthen you.

If you could for one hour be with your divine self—that is,

your outer you and your inner you together in the presence
of God—you would change the whole mood of our generation,
so powerful is this light.

Try; hold nations in the palms of your hands and shine on
them. The big and the little, the little and the big—there is
no scale.

Walk with the great ones. Keep the vigil.

ↄ

I‍T IS TRUE, YOU CANNOT FOR A MOMENT BE FEARFUL, IT IS NOT
the role for a soldier. Attack without fear and you will be
given courage for each fraction of a moment. Courage is what
will steady you; you need to bite into courage and hold tight,
then you will be free from the drill sergeant of discipline.
Only the fearful are disciplined; keep far ahead of your fears,
then you will be calm, protected and completely safe. Only
the confident are quiet and full of success, only they can poke
out their tongues at the drill sergeant who is so full of wind!
Courage is a matter of *élan*. When again in the battle smoke
where all things swell big to frighten the child in you, take
out your little drum and beat it hard and armies of heroes
will gallop with the glint of eternal valor on their helmets, for
is it not an eternal truth that a child shall lead them?

Brave men are childlike.

> *By prayer I do not mean any bodily exercise of the
> outward man; but the going forth of the spirit to-
> wards the Fountain of Life. . . . The natural tendency
> of the poor, rent, derived spirit towards the Foun-
> tain of Spirits. . . . To retire inwardly and wait to
> feel somewhat of the Lord.*
>
> Isaac Penington, 1617

ↄ

IT IS WISE TO KEEP SPIRITUALLY AHEAD OF THE TIMES; KEEP IN the ultimate and fear not! If you can do this you will not be dated and have to go through certain stages of discipline. Not discipline so much as consequences, lessons.

Much has been said of the necessity to get into the thick of life, to "know it in the raw." But that one is fortunate indeed who can stand away from it with such detachment that he can see the weaving pattern; he can escape many knots and tangles; and, too, his critical faculty becomes kinder. There are many ways of learning the same lesson, but shall we not listen to the comfort in the words, "Take my yoke upon you and learn of me, for my way is easy and my burden is light," and is it not the moment to ponder on the inner meaning of "to know God is eternal life"? If we could do more than perceive the truth in these words we could enter now into deathless beauty, timelessness, our immortality.

One of the beneficent gifts of this, your chosen action, this communion with the Spirit, is an escape from many states that savage and ignorant men are heirs to. All that is asked of you is to practice the secret way and see the unfoldment.

When challenged by terror always attack in spiritual action, for in this attack, this action, is your only rest. Attack the first suggestion of fear; how? Try such words as these; say, "Lord, lead thou the way! Lord, I would be thy messenger and as thy messenger I will obey thy words. I will be true, I will be one with thee, I will not surrender to the negative forces, I will not be fearful of the sea of entangling angry emotions. I will step forward following thee, for in so doing I will gather immortal strength. Lord, here I am."

By such a stand of spiritual manhood you will be released from entanglements which you have magnified. Magnify instead the omniscient, the august and mighty power you have within you.

We have told you that your inner you walks in the power of God; you will receive a faint realization of that mightiness by an act of complete faith, a surrender to the holy stillness within.

In these days when time presses and seems to matter so much, perhaps you will be willing to listen to some of the ancient wisdom from an old man.

First, there is an incorruptible *now*.

In broad daylight, eyes wide open, looking at a house, a street, a hill or a common scene of every day—look at your picture with its tendency to stir up trains of thought, of memory, of anxiety, and dissolve it to the eternal moment while you look. That the house grows old, the leaves fall from the tree, that spring comes to renew the world, is not for you to be dismayed about.

No, the eternal moment which is part of your godhood, futureless, without past, gives more beauty to the scene because you are there and yet—are not there! You are in truth and not deceived; you are in pure joy and not made tragic by your thoughts of comparison; you are in peace and not in turmoil.

This is a secret of great value for it will give you spiritual stamina, freedom from regret, and will hold you to your true stature.

. . . What better way to meet conditions than with a timeless courage steadying your heartbeats, inspiring with eternal inspiration your every act? It is as if you took this thing called fear and in its place, fitting perfectly, you placed pure courage. Let us examine this thing called courage. True courage, spiritual courage, is without strain, is relaxed, it is a state not ruffled, it is an outpouring steadiness, it is strong, confident, without effort, a calm benediction—for it comes from within.

We are concerned with keeping you at your full spiritual stature, for by being there you will be eternally safe.

. . . I would like to add a word for I know you may think that when you hear these things on a headachy, distracted day they seem very far removed from your instant, unsolved, and nagging problem. Well, it is not impersonal or cold. See it as the figure of Christ, for he is eternally now, eternally fresh. He is the divine principle. Keep always invisible in the stillness of his invisible presence. You say this is hard? It is not hard! It is a loving awareness; not being blotted out for hours at a time in nothingness. It is not as difficult as being a good student or a laborer in the fields. Instead of falling into the sleep of oblivion that steals away the precious moments, you abide in that beautiful awareness that keeps the instant flaming, alive with joy and peace.

> . . . *And he shall find all that he can ask, and that as deep as the mind of man is able to reach.*
>
>   Jacob Boehme, 1575-1624

〜

AS THE UNSEEN IN YOU IS HELD CAPTIVE BY THE SENSES SO ARE you a prisoner. The loneliness, the loneliness, the loneliness, which is the lot of all who wonder! Those you see about you are ensnared by the noise, the color, the interests of other souls like yourself; they gather together to do away with this loneliness; all these souls, like yours, are seeking release in affairs, in personal experiences; sharing what you call gossip, feelings of patriotism, of endeavor, of art—all so far away from the lonely reality of God. It is as if in a multitude of marching men going with bands, banners and tumult, interested vitally, emotionally in comradeship with one idea to achieve, you turned about right-face and walked back; this is why the road to God is so difficult.

I have heard you ask why it is you forget in the midst of knowing? How is it that you cannot keep yourself in the Presence? How, when you step out of your bed, you are assailed with armies of thoughts and vain imaginings for your busy day ahead? Then you assail and wound yourself with the blows of the daily news and with hurried spirit you go out to your appointed task. "Will this happen? Can I move *this* about?" Things not done delay your plans; stupidities block and anger the spirit, disappointments, sudden hopes, in fact, all the excitement of the day's achievement has kept you far away and made you shallow. Why do I dare say that you are made shallow? Because you are living way out there on the fringes of yourself, even outside of your lines of defense.

Now let me show you how you can meet your day.

On waking wake in joy and plunge yourself into great stillness. Dissolve your universe into thought. Then meet the news, meet the onslaught as if it were the barking of a pack of dogs far away outside of this still park of your estate. Carry this stillness of serene sky, quiet pools, and transcendent beauty with you. Step into the hard reality and you will find that you can see through it instantly when it has been resolved into thought.

The temptation to anger on account of a stupidity, a challenging personality, a shock or disappointment, and all the heavy awkward conflicts are present, but they shrink into their natural and relative places in the divine scheme. They are mere shadows in the beauty of your scene. See through them, past them; they have challenged but not disturbed your eternal serenity. You are living far, far in the future. What you see is the past; oh, my eternal children, this is the way, the truth and the life! This is no idle panacea, this communion, brought to comfort you with ephemeral comfort. No, this is what you asked for; like Moses you struck a rock. It is no idle word, neither is it meaningless that God is power transcendent, and omniscient. Sitting, walking, eating, sleeping, waking with this splendor in your heart, this still Presence will give you complete majestic dominion over all mankind—that disturbing mankind within yourself. If you ask for this it will come like the waters of life from outer and inner darkness. It is clean and still and far and wide and high and deep; it is glorious beyond the feeling of rejoicing.

Wake, then, little, perturbed, anxious, weary, frightened children, and stand released in this holy stillness; then will the picture be fulfilled. Results follow after. Be in a place which brings results.

Now as you have turned against the marching multitude, when you awake each day in renewed confidence you will find that you will not forget so quickly. You will not be snuffed out nor blanketed nor turned to salt by events, disappointments, turmoil, news. No! You will find that this is a principle which quiets the spirit, relaxes the step, enlarges the heart and everywhere brings tidings of great joy. Be therefore Knights of the Holy Grail sanctified, purified, and dedicated. Your sincerity is known, your foibles are known, the inner wishes of your hearts are known. Resolve; marshal your will and your intent, find your purpose and your directions, then will you be sustained and comforted and reminded of the Presence in this holy place.

I was a humble servant, I was a humble voice, I was a coward, and out of hell and torture I was lifted by a thought into this eternal stillness of love and light and power and joy and knowledge and truth.

This kind of knowledge is a thing that comes in a moment like a light kindled from a leaping spark which, once it has reached the soul, finds its own fuel.
Plato, 428 B.C.

WHEN YOU FIRST CAME TO THESE COMMUNIONS WITH ALL the fresh enthusiasm of beginners we knew that though your hearts were good you could not realize, except for brief moments, the majesty and splendor as the gates were opened before you and you were made free. You would forget and be drawn back, closed in and swept away into what you considered reality, and all the alarms and terrors and hurts of your human life would again press close. That which had been awakened in you would then bring you again to seek the reassurance and comfort of the revealing Spirit which only speaks in the silence of the "sovereign shining darkness" and each time of your return you were uplifted and through this heavy flesh you felt the freedom. O earth enshrouded, O pain-imprisoned mortals, while you have the pearl of great price in your hands you look away like distracted children!

In the compelling interest, tenseness and drama on this difficult journey even the assurance and peace are forgotten. This is understandable, for the growth is slow and often you feel far away from the light. The doors seemed locked and closed to you and you become earth-bound again, chained to old habits of thought and action. In spite of this you know that when you come into the presence of the living Spirit, then there are no locked imprisoning barriers. When you leave, waiting for you, ready to sweep in on you, are the racing material thoughts where your minds seem, at present, more at home; even with what you may call the practical strains and needs of life that bring sudden tension when you return to them. We tell you that the path is not flinty, not dangerous, except for your thinking.

Come, and bring your thoughts where they can be held true, so that you can realize how you are held, supported, sustained and protected. This is your safety—your thought, and that thought is the realization of the presence of God here and now, within you, in the life you are living.

The experiences you have had in these communions from the beginning have built up in you a resistance to evil, unconscious to yourselves, but there is a tendency to be satisfied with the feeling of the quality of the inspiration given you in these lovely freedoms. Be not satisfied; hold it, make the resolution to act upon the wisdom that has been vouchsafed you through these answers to your needs, and act accordingly. And the act is forever one and the same thing—stay your mind in Light. Hold, one-pointed to the actual idea of God himself here, now. Hold your gains, hold your spiritual self together, bring all that you know to this one point, and then "the wonders will appear."

How much it takes to remember your Redeemer who liveth in you! But do you not see that we choose either terror or faith, inertia or action, darkness or light with every thought? Your thought is your armor. This is the magic, this is the splendor, this is the resurrection, this is the mystery of life.

Keep touching Reality with the heart; hold your peace!

. . . When we consider the manifold weaknesses of the strongest devotions in time of prayer, it is a sad consideration. I throw myself down in my chamber, and I call in and invite God and His angels thither, and when they are there I neglect God and His angels for the noise of a fly, for the rattling of a coach, for the whining of a door; I talk on . . . knees bowed down as though I prayed to God; and if God and His angels should ask me, when I thought of God last in that prayer, I cannot tell.

Careless Devotions, John Donne, 1573-1631

YOU SPEAK OF THE DISCOURAGEMENT OF DELAY. LET ME reply to this in a roundabout way. Someone has said that nature teaches us everything once; it is indeed a great and ever-present analogy for us to watch and profit from constantly. How often have I told you of the importance of healing away old habits, appetites that are both physical and intellectual! It becomes a dull story and strikes the ear with no response like many urgent warnings. But elimination is necessary to life, just as food is; it is our hungers that have to be transmuted that our spiritual body may live. Long ago it was thought that pain and self-inflicted misery were the way to teach the material spirit of the body a necessary discipline; men seemed to forget that Jesus taught that the body was the temple of the Holy Ghost. We are still taught by pain, though not deliberately self-taught. But the master who overcame all things taught that by the lifting up of the spirit the body was also resurrected; and the discipline of awareness of the Spirit will transmute material desire, intellectual excesses and emotional storms as heated water turns into steam. Chaotic force can be changed to noble uses. Tormenting desire can be turned into creative power of the mind; resentment dissolved and re-formed to understanding. Receive light like a tree. Accept the ever-present beauty that pours out from within, the indwelling Christ.

Yes, this invisible God seems very far away and impractical in times of dullness and waiting; hard to reach and deeply hidden in the center of your being. You try to find him but your outer you is so critical and suspicious, so exacting, that it is difficult for him to manifest in the company of such thoughts. Your success will come in laying aside the critical spirit, in releasing yourself from the sense of outer pressure, in letting go completely all the negations that block the giver of joy and peace, and surrendering to a feeling of fulfillment. *Let your light shine!* Be strong in thought, and that thought locked in immortality is the principle that is deathless—the love of God.

> *Listen to God in silence when we have spoken to Him, for he speaks in His turn during prayer.*
>
> John Peter de Caussade d. 1751

～

AT THIS TIME WHEN THE TRAGEDY OF THE WORLD PRESSES hard, remember that the power of God is upon you. Let it use you—*let it;* do not strive. And let this awareness of the presence of God be like a flame to you, lighting you, warning you, cheering you this day, and all days. It can be for you a pentecost, for you shall speak with new tongues. Open wide and let the power of the Spirit flow through you like rivers of living water, sweeping out all pettiness, all fears, all doubts of self. When you do this you have risen and the new self has been released from the things of the old, the things you have feared and fought against. Through such daily dying you pass beyond the reach of morbid thoughts and entanglements of nagging fears, and each day you can begin as if it were the morning of your life. Become timeless and never bind yourself with age, for the mind as well as the spirit can be kept young, childlike and free. Faith, weak as it may be, can roll away the stone from your door. Rejoice in the new day and go forth with lifted faces and an inner awareness that will shine out from you; an invisible light perhaps, for only those who can see will see it through their own vision.

*God wants only one thing in the whole world, the
thing which it needs; . . . that thing is to find the
innermost part of the noble spirit of man clean and
ready for Him to accomplish the divine purpose
therein. He has all power in heaven and earth, but the
power to do His work in man against man's will, He
has not got.*

John Tauler, 1304-1361

ONE OF YOU SAID, "I BECOME STRANGELY HARD, LIKE ICE; IF I
could only be thawed!" I cannot thaw you but perhaps I
can help. You are going through stages of growth, of thought,
of blossoming. This is real life and real life is in the schoolroom through which we all have to pass. Just remember what
we repeat so often, touch the Spirit, the warm fire within you,
be happy with it and you will "thaw." Keep on opening,
receiving, listening and obeying and use the inner power and
wisdom for every humble thing you do. The problems of daily
life make people ice-bound so they need thawing; the news-
papers, angers, cold self-righteous furies, terrors—all these are
the dangerous elements of human existence and they do things
to your consciousness to harden you, to dismay and disappoint
you and take away your hope while you live in the dreariness
of a man-made world. You will thaw at the eternal touch and
your world will not be man-made, but the world of immortality, now.

Some of you say, how can we do this with our beloveds in
the terror of war? Believe me, you cannot do this without your
beloveds being blessed by it. One soldier wrote recently, "When
I need some strength of mind, some peace some love, I've
only to look close by—within—and there it is! . . . Keep me
in your heart as a source, too, of help, for there isn't any blood

or thunder possible that can destroy a man's soul when he has received power from God from within himself." This comes warm and living from deep experience and loneliness, when he had found the enlightenment he needed to tell him what to do. He asked, and received. Is it necessary for you to be brought face to face with such savagery before you can turn in panic to your only hope of peace and strength?

The purpose of these communions is to try and make you see that it is of vital importance for you to reach up and touch this quiet, still, clean, holy, omniscient place of eternal peace all the time. This is living beside the still waters, here are the green pastures. Abide in the living word and you will yourself to be sustained, comforted and given joy, and so you will help them through their ordeal. There is no time nor space in this realm where you are aware of the Holy Spirit.

We know the Spirit by its victorious tone.

Emerson's *Journal*

❧

THE OUTER YOU, IN ITS FOOLISHNESS AND REBELLION AND suffering bends to the arrows that fly, to the perils and the dangers. But when it surrenders to the inner you whose instinct is for divine reality you are instantly released from the law of sin and death. Therefore when you have to meet the challenge of the world, come—humble, sore, bewildered—and lay thyself aside, this outer self of instant fears, sadness and temptation, and step into thy inner self who welcomes you and leads you to the high altar where all things are renewed, transcended. Here you are released. Have no fear, it is a sacrament indeed.

You have undertaken the great adventure of becoming holy children, sons of God, and you have to go through a sort of untangling to reach this place of communion and awareness.

Be assured that your sole duty is to go within and dissolve by releasing the outer entanglements, to surrender appetites and forbodings. As I have to remind you again the question of appetites is different for each one, both physical and mental; nor must there be resentment and the old sense of duty in the surrender; it is rather permitting a joyful conviction to grow that there is something infinitely more satisfying. Of course there will be conflicts! Who is not familiar with the reasonable —oh very reasonable!—arguments that come rushing to justify the very human desires of mind and body? They must be met with as much gentleness toward yourself as you would meet them when trying to help another, otherwise your instant rebellion will obstruct and delay you. But in the true spirit of surrender, the giving up of everything that has become a burden, is little effort and the reward is instant; all things in this state work for thy good. And not the old idea of good which was a scourge; but the "goodness which is a rapture."

Let thy troubled hearts be at peace in this serene and healing place, for here the Lord Christ will refresh you, here he will lift the heavy burden from your minds and in thy hearts he will breathe renewed joy and quietude. Have faith in practice.

. . . It is not that we do not see the faults, the weaknesses and stupidities; but we waste no time with them for that is all carnal, heavy and human. It is what the outer people are struggling with. We know these things in you, but you are becoming cleansed and purified through these communions; it is the inner you that—being sought—grows in strength to you, and it releases you from the meaningless and savage experiences of the race. "Forgive us our trespasses as we forgive those who trespass against us." Forgive, give over, release. There is great freedom when this is understood.

In spite of the teaching of Jesus we have been taught to hate evil, but that only justifies the more our complete satisfaction in criticism. In such emotional criticism of our friends and enemies we appear better people to ourselves. It is not the way. It is not our business, and instead of freedom we bind the consequences of poisonous hates and resentments to ourselves. We can turn from abstract evil without harm and with a sense of human righteousness. But the human does not hate evil disincarnate; he hates it in a person. Then we ask, "How can I love my enemies?" It would be plain hypocrisy to say we can, or must, do this in the ordinary sense of the word. But the true meaning will appear to you when we say that the outer you cannot love the outer you of another who lives and has his being in the ancient darkness of the race. Instead, come within and while abiding in the conscious oneness with your inner self see and bless with understanding the inner you of that enemy whose outer you is struggling in the dark jungles of his journey, and by thus releasing him, forgiving him, *giving him over,* you help him on his way. This is loving your enemy, this is the brotherhood of man. And there is no sentimentality about it; for only by abiding in the indwelling spirit can you have the so-called human wisdom as well as the divine wisdom to deal with him according to his needs as well as your own. You may have to put him in prison, but watch thy heart in the matter, for out of it are the issues of life! In times of fierce antagonism realize that the enemy is angry thought; fill yourself, without thought of any person, with a sense of infinite love and eternal peace, for thus are all negative things confounded and a table will be set before thee in the presence of thine enemies.

Give freely of thy spirit and judge not; be longsuffering and patient, for when you are kind with the kindness of the spirit to those who are unregenerate, the act frees your own unregeneracy as well. Blessed is he that sees and understands and forgives. Forgive and ye shall be forgiven the trespasses, the darknesses, the things negative which terrify. They are forgotten in this high clear stillness. Love conquereth all things.

> *Q. During these intervals given to interior silence, what does our soul do?*
>
> *A. It ceases discourse and reflections by a free act which suspends them . . . it rests in attentive silence, rather like one who believing himself on the point of hearing music makes himself alert and attentive to what he wishes to hear.*
>
> John Peter de Caussade d. 1751

✍

HOW IRKSOME IS OBEDIENCE! THE OUTER YOU IS THE SPOILED child, it is greedy for new sensation, it runs to bright ribbons or gay music down the street. But no small child grows to man's estate without suffering. It is disciplined by the antagonisms aroused; discipline and obedience are both a mystery and no one arrives at the holy place undisciplined and disobedient. Obedience is irksome for the wild colt and the stubborn ass; why is it necessary? Because the still, eternal law is in divine order. The ignorant and undisciplined and the disobedient perish, for it taketh a thousand to make one. The law is impersonal, inevitable; those who obey and cast aside their rebellious passions are given freedom, protection and joy.

Let us look at man. Every step from childhood, has he not been disciplined? What for? To meet a standard. What is a standard? An ideal goal, an ideal man. The race instinctively knows the inner you—what else is good citizenship, good sportsmanship? What are "men of honor," "men of good breeding" but those who have been trained to a point where instinctively the inner you stepped to the fore and took charge.

What stood up at Agincourt, Crecy? No spoiled, undisciplined men, but men who from childhood were taught obedience.

You speak frequently in common talk of the man you trust in a crisis. What do you trust? That something deeper than he will rise up and take charge. The unseen inner you will always obey.

Now let us ponder. Are you going to be a lazy undisciplined slave to the weaknesses of your outer you? Are you going to let the sleep of forgetfulness steal over your mentality and blunt your keen awareness? Are you going to seek after soft escapes where there is no real rest nor safety nor contentment? Ponder on these things that I speak of in gentle companionship, for a hint is as good as hours of words. There is no finer reward than that which comes from loving obedience! This is what brings rest, security, abundance and love. Here you reach a place out of chaos. Here all things fall into their allotted places, divinely measured.

Now perhaps we can reach an understanding and more will dawn on you by degrees, as you must admit it has in the past. The hint is this; certain it is that he, who, undisciplined, charges life with bit in teeth will meet violence. Violence attracts violence, but so do extremes like weakness, inertia, unawareness and ignorance. The ignorant man often wonders why violence surrounds him but every soul upon this planet is disciplined. Only those who gladly run out to meet it are divinely protected, for they reach a place of safety. It is true that many spiritual people have within them certain unrealized weaknesses; that is why they often suffer and say, "I have not been bad, I have done worthy things—why—why—why?" This is only a hint, for the whole truth cannot yet be understood; but as you open yourselves to a divine guidance your outward self will invite the inward one, in which there is no ignorance, to walk in companionship and will accept the discipline needful with a high heart, for the knowledge vouchsafed will be that then the discipline is light, soon over—over instantly when realized.

Now do not expect hard discipline—rather be there first (in the secret place) in obedience and you will be spared a lifetime. I say to you that when you are obedient you help all those in prison by your freedom, for you are free in your obedience to the divine law, to its will.

I know this is puzzling, but it should enlarge your spirit with heavenly joy. For when you have found it in perception, when you have realized it as you will here in this life, you will free the imprisoned, lift the darkened into light so they will not have to go through violence; you will open the eyes of the blind that they may at last be free to see themselves and you will unstop the ears of the deaf who cannot hear the divine whisper. You will see great wonders come to pass and although the reason behind it all may confound you now, march gaily on up the road obedient with every breath.

I charge you to release yourselves from the last stain of materialism for then only are you protected; I charge you to be forgiving and patient with all persons whether they be stupid, melancholy or evil and to keep your faces always uplifted to the highest intent, for this, above all, releases your life from all violence; I charge you to live in faith, for this will give you a splendor, a light which will be manifest to all the bewildered, the lonely, the harassed—a beacon in the storm. Stand to your full stature, for I bear witness that eternal love can be reached.

When "obedience" is spoken you know what that means; no one can translate it for you. It means seeing how often during your day you can remember him in whose Presence you stand, for by calling him to mind you glorify each moment.

His giving is my taking.

                                    Meister Eckhart, 1260-1327

THERE WILL BE A TIME, AS WITH CHRISTIAN, WHEN YOU WILL come to a gate and your heaviest burden will fall away; it will fall when the realization of the spiritual and unseen life is the only reality. In times of stress that is difficult and that is why these communions are good. In the beginning you came to them through suffering; now you come for refreshment and joy and because through them you find you are strengthened. There is nothing to fear if you stay within in quietness and if your thought is not allowed to slump into the slough of despond. The human story, the alarms, the heavyweightedness is understood. You have your measurement, each one of you. You are protected by your own thoughts because your intent is for perfection, your intent is for grace.

Now follow me; step into this garden surrounded by cloistered arches. Sit here awhile. Lay aside the heavy garment of the world, of darkness and forboding. Put on this shining raiment. Do not look back or look ahead! Do not cling. Walk here in this quiet place, in the flowered stillness; come here to this fountain and drink of these waters, they wash your spirit clear. Here is where you ask that you may receive.

. . . I know what it is to make mental pictures and bury oneself in a mire of one's own making, to be so cowardly one is sickened by a thought of spiritual help. I know what it is not to find my way, how pride and fear and all the negatives lie heavy on the chest and tire to the bone, how the outer you in a material world sweats apace in the heat of the struggle and snatches at quick opportunisms to solve his problem. It is always the same struggle. I know how regrets and shames come in the night to shame again. But do not hang back with your mistakes, it but gives them power. Release in thy heart all things but joy and gladness, simple beauty and pity and under-

standing and forgiveness. That is being vitally and spiritually
active, that is freedom. In your everyday life you cannot yet
hold this quality of spirit all the time; you go up and you go
down, but each time you go higher. Have no fear; step in here
and put on your invisible cloak, and nothing can reach you
from without. You can only reach God in this holy stillness,
in calmness. What is a week, a month, in this august destiny!
Play the part nobly, refuse frantic littleness. Stand at thy
full stature and deny everything that is not of God. Make manifest in your material life the inward surety that is being
breathed into you, and you, in turn, breathe it into your outward existence.

Come unto me, all ye that are heavy laden. Trust not the
eye nor the ear nor the tongue, for I am closer than hands or
feet. Deep in the invisible center . . . here I am. Trust in
me, thy Father; my life I give unto thee. I will lift the weariness from thy heart, despair from thy mind and give thee
peace.

Go forth renewed, refreshed, reborn . . . in confidence.

> *Dost thou love picking meat? Or wouldst thou see*
> *A man i' the clouds and hear him speak to thee?*
>   John Bunyan, 1628-1688

᷍

WE TALK OF FAITH LIKE A GRAIN OF MUSTARD SEED, FAITH
that will move a mountain. Why, if you were a poor
mongrel, a mangy cringing pariah, one touch of this strong
antiseptic faith would heal you instantly, would steady your
heartbeat and thrill you with an ancient courage. Do away with
mongrel thought! I have seen the little made great, the weak
made giants and the fools made wise by this divine elixir.

The men of science tell us that if you lift your hand you

move the planets—ever so little, but a little. Remember the invisible between you everywhere in the realm of the mind. We are all held together so if you go down you drag others down with you; you either glorify the invisible world about you or darken it. No wonder many are helped almost instantly when they come into crystal purity! Hold and keep the invisible substance pure. Don't you know how, when some startling thing happens, some virulent personality rises out of the depths into your life, you feel it? Help to cleanse him by an act of faith; turn loose the fountains and cleanse the air in your outer circle, keep it clear and unsullied. In this atmosphere are you alive, deathless; this is your home. Start your day here, bathe in it, drink deep. Everyone who comes, whether it be a child or a dog, multitudes or a single unhappy soul, people in darkness and despair, you can help to heal. Such is your task—to make the unseen a reality.

Go forth, then, in the Invisible, and by holding and bending every thought and desire to this purpose, yea though you walk through the valley of the shadow, you will be comforted. Open wide and let it pour out, strong, vibrant, still; it is stronger than human life for it is Life, spiritual, eternal, everlastingly renewing. Go therefore into your little world in your humble outer you, go forth—giants! "My peace I give unto you"; it is so real. This largesse is the love you can give your neighbor.

〜

WE HAVE WATCHED YOU ON YOUR WAY; WE HAVE SEEN THE crossroads that tempt you down and away from the straight path ahead. We have seen you stop, puzzled, but you have listened and heard the warning. At last you have come to a place on your journey where your burden is growing lighter, where you can live miraculously, live in freedom, live without fear. Shake yourselves clear of old habits and travel light, as you have been told. Every moment is a challenge to an act of faith, but you have a joy in the companionship of the saints. One more hint—watch your tongue; do not speak from without, make the habit of speaking from within. Then are you safe.

Hold thyself to Thyself and live in splendor; question nothing; be strong and remember you do not walk alone. Frightening thoughts will tempt you down the wrong road, but blow your silver bugle and the walls will fall down before you; let nothing keep you against the wailing wall where they still weep. No—say, "I do not understand what I see humanly, but I know my kingdom is within," and accept gaily. By accepting I mean go out into a dull world, into the shallowness of human life, and see immortality and the grandeur of the human heart. The very people you criticize can betray you by acts of heroism. You touch it wherever you go in your seeing of it. I know all the wrong-headedness and stupidities latent in the human overcoat, the temptations and subtleties that lie in its folds, but the true, revealing, piercing, spiritual gleam will free you from the bondage of your own critical spirit.

Nothing is asked of you but the highest you can reach. Therefore go forth; all the goodness, all the loveliness, all things hoped for are thine if you let nothing bind you. This is the resurrection and the freedom. Go forth on thy way, no one before thee but the Lord Jesus.

. . . You are not altogether aware of the spiritual strength that you have won. We want you to realize it, to concentrate it as through a burning glass on any problem you may have. Read over these things and *make them manifest*. Because of a childish unbelief you do not act upon what you have heard, what you have learned.

Suppose you compare your mind to a cloud; within this cloud is the divine spark—but your awareness of this inward light is intermittent. You can glow with such a fiery faith your cloud will be a blinding light. Since you have found this contact, do what you have been told—bring a fiery enthusiasm and listen to the words roused within. The outer you meets a suggestion of despair—let him shine on it, burn it out! Do not meet it with a soft, wishful prayer, but with a stalwart enthusiasm. The promptings within will voice all your answers to your temptations. Look at lack—fill it. Look at want—supply it. This is no time for spiritual laggards. Remember I am speaking of your inner kingdom, "my words are spirit."

More often than not your mind is filled with unrelated, unfruitful thoughts. It is good practice whether walking or riding or waiting to use those moments to be in touch with your divine fire; to get into action-thought. Use your imagination to see it as a great dynamo. Your fires must not burn low, and in doing this it is as if you put on fuel. Shake yourselves, laugh and play and your thoughts will be charged with flame and power and you will burn up the obstructions, these quaking fears. It may be difficult to believe this while your problem looms, but we can assure you that it is the glorious way, for the tiniest efforts bring results. As evil men are alert, active and sometimes inspired, we tell you also to keep alert, sing your high note and stop the daydreaming which leads you into the dark valleys.

What is being given you is prevision; here at this place in high hope, in scorn of defeat you are being challenged. Accept the challenge gladly, for in the accepting lies success, in this is victory won. Rest on the idea of victory—always!

> *Visible deeds do not increase the goodness of the inner life, whatever their number or dimension; they can never be worth much if the inward process is small or nonexistent and they can never be of little worth if the inner process exists and is great.*
>
> Meister Eckhart, 1260-1327

LET ME TRY TO EXPLAIN A LITTLE WHAT IS GOING ON. WE, because of your desire, have made the effort to teach you not dogmatically, but through suggestions, feelings, love. We try to inspire you by delicate hints to realize your own power. Of course it is difficult, but every time you come to a realization it is a step toward victory. Don't be discouraged by the delays and seeming difficulties and the curious states your human mechanism seems to bring forth in you. You cannot push yourself too fast; be happy, be gay, for it makes it so much easier not to be solemn.

Do not expect to hold great revelations all the time; and one thing beware of—do not drive and scold yourself if you cannot keep your outer you where you want it. This is but a hint to you to take your adventure with an easy confidence rather than a straining eagerness. You have high spiritual moments where the skies have cleared for you; don't be dismayed if you can't keep them clear by your will. There is a rhythm. Remember, as I have told you before, the outer you and the inner you are not separated; the divine you is in you from the beginning. Many men have lived through a life and not known it, because the art of turning the eye inward does not come to all. Neither does education come to all, but those who have it often inspire others in their search for knowledge. The child does not know that he has within himself the potentiality of an educated man; he may go through life and never know it. In the same way you have within you a spiritual giant, undreamed of by your present consciousness. Through your desire you have started your journey inward and according to your desire this spiritual consciousness will more and more reveal itself to you, teach you, inspire you, take charge of you, so that your outer you is absorbed the way the child, ignorant and fearful, is absorbed by the educated man. It is as if you

made room for light; it is as if the amateur became an artist
in touch with the indefinable majesty of his art.

You have accused me of saying at times this is "life and
death important," and that I have contradicted myself by
telling you to restrain too much eagerness.

It is difficult not to sound contradictory in a matter so delicate, so subtle. Suppose we go back to the artist idea; it *is* a
"life and death matter" for the artist to work at five-finger
exercises, but he never becomes an artist if he strains. I am
trying to tell you—and telling you very badly—that a loving
enthusiasm which forgives clumsiness and awkwardness but
keeps happily on is what is required.

It is true I tell you to be eager—not to be eager; to search
with all your heart—and not to make an effort. Here is the
answer—you make an effort not to make an effort, which is
what all great artists do. It is another way of saying in great
action is great peace; and what is most beautiful is that when
you find the great stillness you are in the place where you are
answered.

What is meant is that when you go out into the startle of
daily life—hold the hand of thy Lord. Hold his hand as you
were told. He can be so quickly, delicately pushed aside. It is
indeed a question of "life and death." Hold him close, no one
can go into the arena for you, you go alone with him.

Practice not being startled, scattered by the daily assaults,
bored into daydreaming by long hours of indecision and dullness. Be confident, be radiant, be aware that you do not walk
alone.

*The present hour is the descending God, and all
things obey; all the past exists to it as subordinate; all
the future is contained in it. . . . By lowly listening,
omniscience is for me. By faithfully receiving, omnipotence is for me.*

Emerson's *Journal*

IN THE BEGINNING WE REMINDED YOU THAT THE WAY WAS marked by realizations, that you were to resolve everything to thought and your thought would be made manifest, and now when we look back we find that you have been brought step by step to heights of realization; many so subtle, so faint that at the time your awareness was faint—immature. The whole business of spiritual growth is a development of your conscious realization that thought is the beginning and end of your life, whether it be spiritual or material. In the negative experience where man has refused to look deeper than his five senses and has indulged his appetites, he is bound to meet the full realization of his failures, whether it be in defeat or violence, sickness or despair. And you who have endeavored to seek your life within, will find that your realization cometh in the awakening to the beautiful and freeing knowledge that the thoughts of your inward selection, that is, what you choose to entertain, will be "made flesh." As I said before, think your way out. Believe this; choose your thoughts with wisdom and make your own declaration for this is a high form of that misunderstood word, prayer. Prayer has always been a cup held up to be filled.

Now the purport of this wisdom is to reveal your character to you and in the very depths of the wisdom that will come to you, if you will listen, is contained the truth for your particular problem. Through the eyes of wisdom you will see your particular direction; how and where to use your gifts, how to collect them into your personal galaxy. For example, you will see (when you grow still enough, delicate and sensitive enough in holiness) where you are resentful, where you are forgetful, selfish, wasteful and where you are weak. Instead of sitting in dismay before the array of your lacks of character, receive the divine healing spirit from within and let the fountain of reassuring goodness play in the dry places that are athirst. In this way selflessness, love and consideration come with enlightenment and are constantly renewed until they come involuntarily to stay and become a part of you. Or, and it is nearer the truth, the inner you is called out into your life, and you begin to understand a little what your Christhood means. You begin to realize a little how you are in truth and practice a son of God. This is prayer, for prayer is actually the filling of the want, the lack, the emptiness. It is an action to take in quietness by yourself. As it has been said many times before, you teach your outer you by staying within.

Sometimes when you repeat the great familiar words they will sound stale and uninspired, but they will take on new meaning, and in the quiet they will be redeemed for you. Your part is in obeying the words that are full of power, words that you seek and love; it is not enough that "Love your neighbor as yourself" is a releasing and beautiful concept—you must say to your outer you, "Do not flame, do not burn with angry fire, do not try to justify yourself with 'righteous indignation.' Be still, impersonal, silent." Receive this eternal love and let it pass through you to the outermost limits of your world. Peace beyond understanding is not a pleasant hope nor revery, it must be told this tumultuous outer self. Stand behind and calm his excited or morose personality. It is not enough to perceive a faith that can make whole, you must give it to this frightened child, reassuring and filling with confidence his quailing heart.

Therefore, teach thyself, be thine own master, be thine own physician, find thine own Christ!

> *And thine ears shall hear a word behind thee, saying,*
> *This is the way, walk ye in it, when ye turn to the*
> *right hand, and when ye turn to the left.*
>
> *Isaiah 30: 21*

The way of the mystic is not a drifting in quietness
nor a pleasant emotional release. It is the way of firm
self-discipline, of constant vigilance. It is the way of
the soldier who needs the full armour of God,—
"the sword of the spirit and the spurs of resolution
and action." Or as one has said, "This is no voyage
for a little barque, this which my venturesome prow
goes cleaving, nor for a pilot who would spare him-
self."

                                                    Anonymous

                              ꝸ

AS OFTEN AS WE SPEAK WITH YOU THROUGH THESE LETTERS
you will find there is much repetition; there is bound to
be, for whatever we tell you has its origin in the first word,
the first instruction, the first principle—"Seek ye first the kingdom." We tell it to you in many ways, and yet it all resolves
down to the one eternal truth or principle. In words one
attempts to bring to the remembrance an awareness of the
divine spark within each individual and by stimulating the
imagination and reason reveal the truth of the indwelling
Spirit. Each one of us makes his own choice; it is either the way
of negation, a materialistic philosophy, or the way of the creative Spirit, the Way of Life. "But one thing is needful," he
said, and *"now* is the appointed time." One has said that "two
of the greatest words in our language are *now* and *within.*"

From the first moment of our enlightenment we are given
complete freedom, but one of the hardest things for us to
learn is the eternal vigilance that is necessary to preserve it.
He who would "bring into captivity every thought" to the
obedience of the Christ within has set himself the first task,
the first self-discipline. Who does not know the temptation of

yielding to an emotional upsurging that hardens first into a destructive thought and is so swiftly followed by the spoken word! On the very edge of such a moment of violence there is only one thing to be done; turn instantly about, run within to your high tower and give that dark cloud of boiling emotions (so reasonably justified) to the Almightiness within and while you wait in quietness you will be gradually aware of the transmutation of this human steam into spiritual wisdom and understanding. This is not repression, this is release, this is turning destructive power to creative use, this is true freedom.

Stand in the light and let all the old garments fall away from you, then you shall walk through the fiery furnace unscathed; harbor no thought that will burn. That is your sacrifice to your day, to your time; that is laying down your life. Lay down the vain imaginings that waste and destroy, lay down appetites, those of thought as well as those of the body, and stand clothed in pure spirit, released from the human turmoil, and you will be uplifted high over panics, hatreds, ignorances and alarms. These are the acts of faith and your faith will make you free.

Yes, walk in the garments of immortality now. Do not take on too much the suffering of the world, for the concept is not only too large to understand but is now beyond us. Trusting is part of your role; trusting in high hope, in peace and confidence. Wear these garments of joy without fearful anticipations, look upon the quiet of the hills, of a candle untroubled by the wind; be very, very simple, very uncomplex, very natural in the eternal sense. Keep in the storm center, safe, a power for victory, healing and peace. Be aware of eternal values as against material values, be spiritually intelligent, keep the "naked intent" and *never forget your direction!*

All things in nature are equally incredible.
                              Alfred Lord Whitehead, 1861——

YES, THERE SEEMS TO BE A HEAVY DISMAYING DELAY IN THE outer world, as if the waters of material life were in heavy tide and the times were frozen. And yet you, as children of the Way, have been secretly freed from fear as you have advanced in your invisible selves. The paradox is puzzling to many who journey upon this road, that great revelation and joy often cometh in times of seeming darkness, obstruction and difficulty. In periods of confusion those who live in the invisible while in the visible world can be as yeast, the ferment, the center of the light which is illuminating the dark places, because they remain in peace and are quietly and gently instructed. And by instruction I mean the only form it could take, that of feeling the actual Presence, the reality of the helping guiding spirit.

As you well know, when novices attempt to push forward through their own effort and fresh enthusiasm the world of reality opposes. This is true in art and all human endeavor— that when a positive move is made an obstruction is met. The question then is, Will the challenge dismay and discourage? In the material world the successful ones are not dismayed but gather more strength, win more victories. But the young soul with its new perceptions half revealed, a little overconfident because he is not on guard against the outer you, goes down in a cloud of chilling doubt, for the world is grim indeed to those sensitive souls just awakening. When you go beyond the point of perception, the burden is lifted for the first time. Remain steadfast! Return to childlike simplicity and doubt not. Are you not aware that there is a no-man's-land between your periods of invisible at-one-ment, your holy communion, your sense of reliance in these heavenly moments, and the contact with the impinging material world with its laws of time and place, events and confusions? It is indeed hard to remain there and *remember across* the no-man's-land to this place of creative power and serenity. What has happened, and why you have felt the protection of peace, is that the no-man's-land is narrowing, you remain closer to your place of safety and you are able to bring beams of light to your material world.

You have asked to be spiritual beings; do you know what spirituality is? It is a loftiness, a sustaining, august, fiery, yet still presence. Can you carry this feeling across no-man's-land and hold it in your spiritually-evaporating outside life? Whatever happens, stand in thy full spiritual stature and deny everything that is not of God; nothing will then have power over you except your highest conception.

> *By attaining the height of meditation we gain fulness of rest. Returning to the root means rest. . . . and the return according to destiny means the eternal; knowing the eternal means enlightenment. The holy man attends to the inner not to the outer. All things spring up without a word spoken.*
>
> *Who by unending discipline of the senses embraces unity cannot perish. By controlling the vitality and enducing tenderness he can become as a little child. There is a Being wondrous and complete; before heaven and earth It was. Therefore the holy man sits with a liberated mind.*
>
> *Selections from Lao-tze, 604 B.C.*

〜

YOUR WORLD IS INVISIBLE, THE WORLD OF YOUR SPIRITUAL life within; but invisible also is the world of rumor, racial fears, ignorances, the greed of multitudes, public opinion and human passions. All these are invisible. So are creative inspiration, honest endeavor and integrity. Invisible also is the intent which makes the true servant of medicine, that which is behind the long hours and personal sacrifice; all this is faith invisible. Many who see a sword see but a blade of sharpened steel; but it is a symbol of anger, pain, annihilation and woe. Those who look and are held captive *out there* by what they see are amazed and bewildered when invisible forces suddenly focus into an event. They are startled and disturbed when the hidden forces *the mind has qualified* are manifested in action.

You who from desire for truth and eternal beauty have stepped out upon the great adventure are coming out of that strange captivity, the prison of ignorance, and when you realize the invisible while in the visible, the incarnate in the carnate, the Holy Ghost in flesh and blood, spirit in matter, thought back of the material world, you have learned your first lesson. Have pity upon the tortured soul who has been deformed by that which is silent within him. Because of the invisible world of mind and thought we can reach one another; and because of the omnipotence of the Holy Spirit we can make gifts of healing and peace, without a word. In this way we obey the second commandment of Christ.

The invisible is the only reality; honor is invisible, so is love; yet they last and all else crumbles and changes. Go forth, then, beloved invisible ones, knowing that you have touched the only reality. The place where you now stand you have reached through listening, following an invisible desire, a vision which pierced the dark. There is great tenderness for you when your feet are weary and your shoulders are tired of the burden and your emotions smother you with fear. Ill-smelling winds blow upon you from those places where liberty has been imprisoned, honor defiled and greed unmasked; you hear it in voices, it sweeps across the daily news, and meets you at every turning. You are in a sea of invisible negatives if you look down; all ancient, all insistent. They challenged me and my father and my father's father and they challenge

you. Face them! For all these things are met at some time.
Face them and then look up and see them no longer. He that
dwelleth within is the light of the world and can shine through
your every act if you will but obey, live in his presence and
keep illumined in his light.

Therefore shine and take great heart whether there are
wars or rumors of wars, alarms and confusion and all the high
cry of chaos, for through him abiding in you you can fulfill
your privilege of life and bring light into darkness.

Keep your mind a lighted lamp.

> *When men doubt it is often because they are trou-*
> *bled by density, what is firm to touch or appears hard*
> *to the eye. The infinities of smallness they know*
> *nothing about, such as the solidity of gases or the vast*
> *spaces between the universes which make a lump of*
> *sugar. They trust their limited perceptions of the*
> *world about them and are entirely ignorant of the*
> *rapidly changing conceptions of matter. Men need to*
> *look more, not less, to science and such men as Ed-*
> *dington and Jeans who are not confounded by the*
> *visible universe.*

Anonymous

～

SOMETIMES IN MOMENTS OF TEMPTATION WHEN ONE IS
enveloped in the fog of doubt and disbelief, there is a
lowering of the bars which guard you from fear so that meditation is difficult. That is understood. It is as if a noisy crowd had
entered the room and your spirit of communion had been
pushed to the uttermost edge and then lost. But these things
happen during the pilgrimage and your safety is in knowing
that underneath all temporary confusion lies your intent. Even
if you sit with mind racing and you scold yourselves for being
ensnared by nonessentials, let me assure you that by sitting

obediently, even though your mind is concerned with trifles, the act is a prayer in itself and you are given the privilege of holding to your direction until you come through the fears or perplexities. In this way you go on your everlasting journey in eternal life and glory immortal. Be more aware of the transcendental loveliness in simple acts; here you are, two or three people sitting together in quiet with a desire to place themselves in the way of learning—to be at one with immortality, but I tell you that though your minds wander and at times the experience seems meaningless, you have lifted banners against the power of darkness. This is turning toward the Light of the world.

Let us speak for a moment about discipline, but discipline as a beneficent force, which is ultimately revealed as involuntary strength in time of need. You have been told many things to which you have responded with loyal belief, but you have not acted upon them with all your might and main. The endeavor to apply these promises to your insistent daily lives has been spasmodic. But surely you have seen already that the good to be received or extracted from this adventure is obedience to the law. You have seen the power and the force created by the power of the sword; there is a certain perfection, however misguided, in the application of the laws of Caesar in the body politic. Let us examine the antithesis of that law; first, deep centralization and individual responsibility to the inner voice. You know the results of unorganized living. You know, too, that the organized disciplined forces of Caesar are gained through self-sacrifice and discipline, ruthless though they may be. To overcome the world (the power of Caesar) one must organize and discipline oneself, but where he has seeds of defeat sown in healthy ground, you have victory inherent in your enterprise. Your work is to be strong and clean enough within through self-discipline to bring to completion the work that has been given to you.

You ask how? Again we tell you, control appetites; appetites that rise from personal desires that are unworthy of the spirit, as well as the appetites of the body. A problem presents itself; nothing is trifling, therefore bring the serene clarity of intelligence, that high spiritual intelligence, to bear on it. Shall I do this or that? and you will be told the way to face because your intent is to obey righteousness rather than to drift in the lassitude of unrealized potentialities. The time has come to break into light, and to keep this light illumined calls for self-restraint, sacrifice and self-examination.

This country is today paying a dreadful penalty for the neglect of youth by parents and teachers who do not believe in discipline. This disservice cannot be overestimated for the timeless truth is that this planet is a schoolroom for discipline, and the beginning of that knowledge should come when a child is hardly aware of cause and effect, of the waiting consequence. The results of mistakes, poor judgment and youthful enthusiasm can be taught with wise, firm gentleness and even a sense of humor, but this law must be taught in order to prevent the unhappy bewilderment and suffering with which youth will meet frustration and injustice when he crosses the first threshold into his world. Self-discipline is the armor of God and can be taught as easily as the discipline on the athletic field. If it is not, then when he leaves the license of home and school he has to face the pain and misery of the law of trial and error, whether swift or slow in coming. Strong, self-controlled, gay, vital; not self-indulged, destructive, satiated and unhealthy minded, ignorant of "the laws of sin and death."

I speak of youth, but as these truths are ageless so are you, they belong to you as to the very young, you are still very young in this adventure. Be vigilant, keep eternally alert, keep in the quiet estate and be always aware that you walk with God.

O Thou, who by Mind everlasting rulest the world,
Maker of land and sky, who orderest Time to flow from
the beginning, and Thyself at rest, makest all things
move; whom no external causes urged to fashion the
work of fluctuating matter, but the innate Form of
the Highest Good, beyond all rivalry. Thou deducest
all from a heavenly pattern, Thyself most beautiful,
guiding a beautiful universe of Mind, moulding it to
that Image, and commanding its perfect parts to com-
bine for the perfection of the whole. Thou bindest
the elements by numbers, that cold should match with
heat, and dry with moist, lest the pure flame should
fly off, or the heavy things overlay all lands.
In like manner Thou bringeth into being Souls,
and the lesser lives, yoking sublime to frail vehicles,
which by a kindly law Thou makest to return to Thy-
self by virtue of their native fire.
Grant, O Father, to our minds, to climb to that
august abode, grant us to visit the Fountain of the
Good, grant that, finding the Light, we may open wide
and fix on Thee the eyes of our souls. Scatter the mists
and the heaviness of the earthly mass, and shine out
with Thine own splendour; for Thou art the Serene,
Thou art the tranquil resting place of the steadfast;
to behold Thee is the aim. Thou art at once the
beginning, the carrier, the guide, the pathway and
the end.

Boethius, A.D. 475

THIS IS A TIME FOR REDEDICATION, IT IS A TIME TO LIVE AT your spiritual height. Do all you can to keep free from negative excitements; rather be open to quiet, powerful faith. Indeed, it is through your silences that the flaming powers press. It is difficult with our limitations and the human scale to comprehend the majesty of the spiritual power within; it is a faculty to make the instant flaming, and these holy, immeasurable powers are only trusted to you when you are universal, selfless. Lay down anxiety, lay down impatience, lay down frustration; clear the heart and seek ye first the kingdom. I cannot tell you how to take yourselves in hand, for that mental and spiritual discipline is the part a man must play himself in seeking the kingdom, as I said before; but you can keep a retreat like a pool in the rapids; or, to make a better image, be like the iceberg which is seven-tenths under water. When you learn that seven-tenths of you must be still and calm and in control, while three per cent is in active life you will have some conception of the grandeur of the attempt you are making. In the old way three-tenths was with the source of inspiration of your life and the seven-tenths was with—well, shall I say it!

This is only friendly talking, trying to bring to your remembrance what is yours. May I say here that the mind cannot remember easily when it is full of criticism; you cannot afford to take umbrage, to have prejudices, nor hold to yourself these violent human emotions which flare up in human contacts. Let them go and dwell in the source of all love, infinite love. Now "infinite" you have heard before, so often that it has been pinched down into a meaningless term. But when you begin to get the savor of it, "love," following after, is revealed to you in its full sense. Then the power of God Omniscient becomes yours. Prepare yourselves to be sons of God, rise to your full height and live most of your life in spirit while in the material world.

. . . The discipline of the body and the spirit is an exercise as old as time. The conflict of body and spirit, joy and sorrow, has been an accompanying mystery; the dawning of man's consciousness to light has been a way of suffering, but the journey has not been in vain for the victories of the past are still in the race and those who have conquered are with you and have helped to make the journey safe, to hold your spiritual self together, to keep your divine awareness that you might not slip into the waters of forgetfulness nor the alluring forest of false dreams of beauty. Therefore, in the insistent, dismaying clamor of need you must invent, each for himself, his own methods— though of course the best of all ways is with life itself.

I will give you a talisman to use in times of pressure, of drabness, of temptation. Say, "There is no measured time at this place, no future, neither is there a past. I am in the eternal moment, the limitless, infinite, now. My spirit is deathless, immortal, and through it I am in touch with all wisdom, all beauty, all goodness. In this eternal now I rest sustained, supported, comforted." All is contained in the present, eternal, moment.

See your appointed position in the great concept, in this eternal moment; for you are bigger than the limitless ocean, or the planet, or the planetary system, or things past or things to come. Carry in august stillness your soul as you are carried about by your body with all its slyness, weakness and tendencies which lead to oblivion. Awake to your eternal moment.

> *If thou wear the hair shirt, fasting bread and water, and if thou saidest every day a thousand pater nosters, thou shalt not please Me so well as thou dost when thou art in silence and sufferest Me to speak to thy soul.*
>
> Margery Kemp, 13th Century

ᕙᕗ

LIFT YOURSELVES AGAIN, LIFT YOUR SPIRITS HIGH! IT IS SO TRUE that it is not a question of fighting but rather a need of lifting, offering a gay and happy spirit in worship. There is discipline required in a stand against appetites for they are subtle and return, when you are unaware, for the onslaught;

and as I have said so many times, it is not only the physical appetites which tempt, but there is a greed of the tongue for those idle words of which he spoke. There are destructive satisfactions in words which fly from the tongue tinged with malice; there are appetites for self-justification and enjoyment in resentment and hot storms of anger. When we realize that there is a mental gluttony for such emotional reactions and a dark pleasure in such indulgence—then we can begin to deal with them. The next time you are tempted by any greed of body or mind, by humanly justifiable anger or quick resentment, repeat to yourself as quietly as you can his words, "*I* am the way!"—or just the great word, "Omniscience!"—and see how the boiling cauldron of heavy poison can be transmuted to light steam which will evaporate in the blue. You will be freed, your mind cleared, your body will feel lighter because your spirit has been lifted. I can promise you a great joy from such obedience, for that is true discipline, that is dominion. Will you succeed the first time? I do not know. Does that matter! Lift your spirit and you will hear the guiding voice and know the joy that is fulfilling.

Do not be cast down by world events for much of the turmoil is beyond your comprehension; do not dwell on the angry clamor but stand in stillness with a lifted heart, for every soul can be a channel for an .inpouring flood of truth and beauty and so contribute toward the victory of the spirit.

Let us return to the image of no-man's-land about which we have spoken before. Do you not begin to see that coming to the spiritual well through your desire is half the story? But it is very important that when you leave the revealing sustaining source you carry across this no-man's-land into the vital personal practical conditions of everyday your well-filled water jars from the well of life. Carry your inspiration and hold it. Do not let it be spilled by the too vital interest of the outer you in its life on the outside. If a man has no source of inspiration within himself from which to gather strength and lives only in the world of appearances, he receives no help from the inner life and depends entirely upon his senses and must be forever surrounded by people and stimulated by the events of his world. But lurking in his subjective consciousness are appetites which are savage and which sweep him into all kinds of storms.

Therefore when you can cross no-man's-land without forgetting, and keep within your spiritual world while among people, when you are at play or at work, when you are spiritually awake to this extent, then you use the savage forces to your own ends and they are literally changed into power and inspiration for you. This is indeed dominion! This no-man's-land must eventually disappear because you will *remember it away* through the continual awareness of the presence of God.

Practice being fully illumined while at your daily tasks and pleasures, fully conscious of your godhood as a child of God.

Thou art to keep thyself in this silence and open the door that so God may communicate Himself unto thee, unite with thee, and then form thee unto Himself. The perfection of the soul consists not in speaking, nor in thinking much on God, but in loving him sufficiently.

Miguel de Molinos, 1640-1697

᷎

IF I TOLD YOU THAT EVERY TIME YOU PRESSED YOUR FINGER ON a given spot the wishes of your heart would be fulfilled, you would come here and press your finger on this spot. There is reality in doing a sensuous thing that you can feel. But if I told you that you could do the same thing with your mind, at once there would be a strange barrier.

This childlike lesson illustrates the whole teaching of

Christ; his spirit must be felt as this touch is felt, then you
have control. You feel this reality of the flesh, but it appears
that when you are asked to touch with the mind, a lost feeling comes because man is so constituted that it is difficult for
him to shape his imagination so that it is as one-pointed as
this feeling of physical contact. To tell an ordinary man he
can touch a spirit with his mind bewilders him; even you who
have been trained in this way of life realize how far away you
are from the practice of being in actual contact. And yet the
traffic of daily living is carried on through thought, though
even the presentation of the idea confuses the average man.

There are currents of thought that flow in all directions,
and you can touch a layer, a sort of strata of impulses and be
caught and held captive. An irritating presence concentrates
the finger of the mind on a layer of dislike and its attending
mutations. Because of the pleasure of dislike the mind is held,
the contact is easy. Again the mind touches the current of
material success. You hear that success breeds success; why?
Because the flush of excitement, pleasure, gaiety *involuntarily*
keeps the finger in contact. So it is with evil; you can touch it
with all the passions. In fact, once started in the negative, and
more familiar layer, the concentrated finger of the mind is
held fast, touching these unseen realities.

The question is, have you the will necessary to make you
one-pointed toward the spiritual impulses? Perhaps not as
yet; and that is why our sympathy is profound and long-suf-
fering, because you are asked to transcend all known experience. You are asked to believe in the invisible, in something
beyond all known experience. We ask you to make as real as
the touching of your finger in the physical contact this other
experience—and that is to keep the finger of the mind on
this thought of awareness. Awareness of the Presence in oneness with your inner you; to be aware of him about you and
in every activity of your daily life. This taxes all your forces.

It is hard, with everything flowing against you, snatching at you, to do this. And yet you have already known a curious breaking through the clouds, glimpses of a great reality that can be sustained. It is as if you saw a shaft of light so golden, so crystal clear, so unlike any light of your experience that you were struck dumb, and even while you looked, it had gone, and in trying to reconstruct it you had dulled it.

But these are indeed glimpses of the Light of the Spirit; be not faint-hearted. Turn to it; stretch out the finger of your mind and touch this light; touch it, touch it all through the day and it will clear the mind of vain imagining, of fear thoughts. It will empty the subcellars of lurking fears; it will keep you from overstraining. Don't live like waltzing mice in a cage; wake up, stop wherever you are and touch with your mind this high state, this high spirit, this light *where you are!*

Who is master? The world or you? It is the eternal struggle; the world, so dramatic, so exciting; the Spirit, so gentle, so . . . *still.*

> *Not thanks, not prayer seem quite the highest or truest name for our communications with the Infinite, —but glad conspiring reception, reception that becomes giving in its turn, as the receiver is only the All-Giver in part and in infancy. I cannot, nor can any man, speak precisely of things so sublime, but it seems to me the wit of man (his strength, his grace, his art) is the grace and presence of God. It is beyond explanation. When all is said and done, the rapt saint is found the only logician. Not exhortation, nor argument becomes our lips, but paeans of joy and praise. . . . It is God in us which checks the language of petition by a grander thought. In the bottom of the heart it is said: "I am, by me, O Child! this fair body and world of thine stands and grows. I am; all things are mine; and all mine are thine."*
>
> Emerson's *Journal*

> *What is't to live, if not to pull the strings*
> *Of thought that pull those grosser strings whereby*
> *We pull our limbs to pull material things*
> *Into such shapes as in our thoughts doth lie?*
>
> Samuel Butler, 1835-1902

ᔪ

LET US CONSIDER TOGETHER THIS OUTER YOU, DISTRAUGHT melancholy, lonely, hypnotized by his own states, without judgment, sound asleep in inertia—mental inertia. In spite of this you know now that it cannot completely possess you. You are being awakened gently, but wisely, to a realization of certain elements within you—traits which make for delay. They are superficial and are not to be dwelt upon; you are not asked at this moment to examine your faults for longer than it takes to be aware of them. The overcoming will be instant when you eliminate from your mind all thoughts and emotions which benumb, frustrate and weave cobwebs.

I am attempting to reveal to you the simplicity and beauty of the unfoldment which has been going on since this new phase has come into your life, largely through your own efforts, a thirsting after righteousness. But it will be of no value if there is too great a sense of effort, of duty to perform. It is an attempt, rather, to awaken the joyful, thrilling spirit of the quest. Meet the challenge—the dreary, seemingly meaningless challenge—of material life with joyous enthusiasm. "Knock and it shall be opened unto you," but knock gaily! In all art, on the high selfless plateau where genius walks, those who know will tell you the path is one of seeming delays. Yet they *asked with industry,* and if you examine their lives you will find such industry and hard work (the actual creating) was not hard work, but a joyful knocking, asking and receiving.

Look upon these days as you would a game of chess: this move, check; this move checkmate, reset. Therefore be not too engrossed with the idea of check, but take the human disappointment and make it, by the alchemy of your spirit, a girder in your character; give no check importance. Your journey from now on should be one of great beauty; not a seeking God out of dark jungles, coming occasionally from a human state into a divine one, but rather one where you will only be happy in his presence and you will hardly step out of it to do your daily tasks; you will carry it with you involuntarily.

Obey your inward voice, but whatever discipline you put upon yourself the fasting must be more joyful than the material appetite satisfied, otherwise it is a waste of time. It must give you pleasure, for by such experiences, this dedication of the befogging, dulling appetites, you will make way for living inspiration. It is of no use if you do not enjoy it more than the satisfied senses. Where are the appetites satisfied in the past of your lives? They are gone, nothing. But the spiritual knockings and attempts, however feeble, are here, they have never been lost. That is why you are where you are, though your brain and spirit are still clogged and the instrument is too fine to be held back by the delayers, the heavy garments of appetites. And by appetites I do not mean normal enjoyments and pleasures, but those things, peculiar to each one of us, which rule us and not we them: almost anything that we cannot drop instantly when the bugle of our spirit blows. Psychic inertia plays a part here.

And so let nothing degrade, let nothing bind, let nothing thicken you nor weigh you down. By the fun of the quest and the laying aside of these pleasurable burdens—in the bearing of which there is no freedom—your spiritual body will take on spiritual enthusiasm and power, and your physical body, health. And so remember the part you play in this must not be one of joyless drudgery, it is that through a secret prompting you follow the voice of beauty.

I worshipped Him the oftenest that I could, keeping my mind in His holy presence. . . . I found no small trouble in that exercise, and yet I continued it. . . . without troubling or disquieting myself when my mind wandered involuntarily. . . . Even in the height of my business I drove away from my mind everything that was capable of interrupting my thought of Him. . . . When we are faithful to keep ourselves in His holy presence it also begets in us a holy freedom wherewith we ask the graces we stand in need of.

Those whose spirits are stirred by the breath of the Holy Spirit go forward even in sleep. If the vessel of our soul is still tossed with winds and storms let us wake the Lord, who reposes in it, and He will quickly calm the sea.

He lays no great burden upon us; a little remembrance of Him from time to time; a little adoration; sometimes to pray for His grace, sometimes to offer Him your sorrows, and sometimes to offer Him thanks for the benefits He has given you, and still gives you, in the midst of your troubles. He asks you to console yourself with Him the oftenest you can. Lift up your heart to Him even at your meals when you are in company; the least little remembrance will always be acceptable to Him. You need not cry very loud; He is nearer than you think.

Brother Lawrence, 17th century

I WANT TO SEND YOU SOMETHING WRITTEN BY ONE WHO HAD great wisdom and knew suffering nearly two centuries ago: "All rests in the feelings and emotions of the heart; they are like great, living currents—hot waters and cold waters, boiling, liquid emotion or iced and frozen secret feeling. How resentment freezes itself and keeps fresh and alive in ice! All is feeling—terrible, stark, animal, feeling. Transmute it with love, for love changes emotion to another state; it melts ice and changes fire to the cool peace of thought. So watch the ebb and flow of emotion and by holy concern and gentleness you will be given mastery so that you will hold nothing in your heart that will boil or freeze. Empty thyself of feeling which is not of truth and which makes slaves of men. Resent not, anger not, allow no pestilential humors to defile thy place or fill thy day with a heaviness in thy breast; empty at once the unclean spirits which come with secret venom—it can be done. Remember, 'for Thy gentleness hath made me great.' Be on guard and watch the temptation of thy feelings to judgment, fill thyself with the guardianship of Love Itself and walk among the dark and bewildering thickets of men and women who are suffering their own burdens of malice and evil, and you will help release them; and by so much will you bring the kingdom of heaven nearer."

I am sure the time has come when you realize that by so much as you have lifted yourselves up from the subjective mud of swift emotional condemnation, criticism and resentment, so much do you realize your escape. And the time will come when these almost involuntary storms of human response will sicken you instantly, you will know that they are chains and cast them away forever. But the casting out means vigilance; it does not mean you cast them out and go about your day in lazy contentment; no, you will learn to rest in vigilance. It is a forever thrusting upward, forever reaching, expanding, growing and being everlastingly aware of that which is within in relation to that which is without, and the relation of that which is without to that which is within. You begin to see the importance of this vigil; how concentrated, how powerful, how impersonal and how stern. Indeed, it is the way of life or death every moment. And yet it is the easiest way, the happiest way; the road to eternal life. Sins are the veils and chains and heaviness that keep your feet in the swamps; fear is the great delayer, weakness the procrastinator. Fight the good fight and be shriven of all nonessentials. Catch the idle moment and retrieve it to everlasting glory and joy.

You have said that I am stern. No; but dear children, it is good to ponder on those who have disciplined themselves to mastery. We do not expect to be understood at once, it is rather that again we make comparison with the amateur, who we feel has not given full measure. Not that one must wear a hair shirt or sandals—life gives us those anyway—nor must one make a fetish or duty of this adventure; but I suggest that because the fight is so tremendous, the better trained and more disciplined the troops, the more wonderful and swift the results. These are days to travel light, to be mobile, for to be in God's presence as a true son, it is well to be unhampered. The yoke is easy, the burden is light and heaven is here and now if we deal with the fogs of our own making that obscure our paths with sternness and in quiet. For every effort there is great reward in joy and peace. So go thy way—perfect in intent.

I will add a postscript. No, our friend is not stern, he writes in answer to a need. Again I say it must all be without too great a sense of effort—like perfect balance or technique. Perhaps it is a little like being in love—when you had rather be in the presence of the beloved than anywhere else. Not effort, but an awareness which keeps you where you belong. For the beginning and end of life is the discovery and the holding and the making manifest the reality of the unseen Christ. How can he be made real when uninvited?

৵

YOU ARE TROUBLED BECAUSE YOUR MINDS ARE CHAOTIC; OF course they are, everyone's is at this time. No one was ever spared fear, vain imaginings, hopelessness or all the other dreary things that present themselves to challenge each valiant one who makes a stand for truth. No one is spared, and we can only repeat the same instructions and suggestions we have given you from time to time; step back into the invisible and put on your cloak of immortality. As you well know each one at intervals goes through the times of the wilderness when it seems impossible to find the well of living water, even in the moments of quietness when one goes to seek it. Know that this happens to everyone. Some of that sense of lack is due to the temporary condition of the body which rises up to confuse our minds and blur our vision. The mind is responsible for the rest of the dryness and discouragement. I do not mean just an idea, but the pressure of outer conditions upon your outer you and the manner in which you interpret the world of the senses to yourselves. Self-deceit and self-pity go hand in hand and suck one dry of inspiration. They will stand in the pathway and confuse your progress. But do not strain nor make a mountain of your heaviness of spirit; keep the balance, for when down in the heavy flesh the subtle body tempts the soul with a sense of defeat. Then is the time to lift up gaily and press on.

Another secret is to fill your reservoirs with light in times of well-being, so that when unease to body or mind steals in like a thief you have the defense of the sword of the spirit which is light indeed. Here is a hint. You think you desire to put aside a small part of each day for the divine appointment, and yet your mental appetites make it impossible of accomplishment. Many of your defenses are down, not through bodily discomforts, but through an unordered rhythm. To some this idea of order irritates the mind, but that is a false suggestion from your outer you; for order, alertness, awareness of the divine companion is rest.

Do not make this a task, it is merely bringing order out of chaos. Begin the day by speaking his words, for this washes away stains from the outer you as you would wash your body; it brings the inner you to the fore, that inner you that will teach you. You have within you the power to make your days brilliant.

On thy brow, on thy lips, in thy ears, in thy heart is the Word. Keep thyself gentle and tender, for it is the way of peace.

> *Are we, in pursuing the mystical outlook, facing the hard facts of experience? Surely we are. I think that those who would wish to take cognisance of nothing but the measurements of the scientific world made by our sense-organs are shirking one of the most immediate facts of experience, namely, that consciousness is not wholly,* nor even primarily *a device for receiving sense-impressions.*
>
> *Science and the Unseen World,*
> Arthur Stanley Eddington, 1882-1944[2]

[2] The roman section is the editor's.

STRANGE AND SURPRISING ELEMENTS ARE IN ALL OF US, beyond our understanding and largely unknown to us— wisely so, for we can only bear the knowledge when revealed to us little by little. Therefore when you find yourselves storming and fretful, tempted to despair by an unexpected revelation, examine it coolly and then pray. Prayer and intelligence, intelligence and prayer. Out of the race have come sayings so supercharged with truth that you would be awakened in a flash if you were sensitive enough to realize their full content. One is, "God helps those who help themselves" and it has become such a commonplace that hardly anyone hears it. But if you can hear it, you will receive deep satisfaction. The questioning, the self-examination, is not a fretful conscience nor a stricken, anxious tidying of the mind. It should be rather a simple question, "Have I this day realized who I am, where I am going, how much I walk alone, how much I walk not alone? How much have I listened? How much have I realized? Is my shield polished to hold off the poisoned arrows of life's dangers and alarms? Can I hold my soul within my soul? Can I be awake to the divine whisper or am I sound asleep? Am I strong, built on a foundation of silence? Am I myself, a son of God, one-pointed, using the wisdom, the knowledge and the inspiration vouchsafed me to live with my fellow men in the troublesome world of confusion, despair and baffling mysteries? Am I vigilant so that when false or sly emotion and sentimentalities sweep over me I can rise above them and see them revealed in all their dangers? What do I want, then? What is my journey? How far have I stepped this day, this hour?

These questions are some of the safe tools; clear and clean your minds with them and you will indeed be illumined and safe in a terrifying world.

Simple exercises are good for this time, and simple images are quieting to the mind. Stand naked, free of all things, greeds and appetites; keep a balance, but keep free of all things. Even while working in groups, keep free of entangling details; keep faithful with quiet, every moment counts. Allow no treachery of thought; walk in the garments of immortality now; keep invisible and indeed have no vain imaginings of fear or doubt. Trusting is part of your role; trust in peace, merriment and confidence. Wear garments of joy without fearful anticipations. Look upon the quiet of the hills, early morning light, a candle untroubled by the wind and let them be to you reminders of your task. Keep in the very center, safe and a power for victory, healing and peace. Keep aware of eternal values as compared to relative values. Keep your naked intent and never forget your direction. By this one thing is meant, live in the awareness of the love of Christ for you, for by so doing you obey his word and give light and peace to the world through him.

> *Let the soul banish all that disturbs; let the body that envelops it be still, and all the frettings of the body, and all that surrounds it; let earth and sea and air be still, and heaven itself. And then let the man think of the Spirit as streaming, pouring, rushing and shining into him from all sides while he stands quiet.*
>
> Plotinus, A.D.[1] 205

∽

YOU CAN COMPLETELY DISSOLVE AND BLOW AWAY THE CLOUD of anxiety if by your concentrated one-pointedness you keep aware of the power of the Spirit. Let there be an awareness so deep it is as if it were in the center of a block of granite, secretly hidden, but held fast. The discomfort of fear will

[1] In this translation of the selection from Plotinus by C. Bigg, the word "Soul" is used instead of Spirit.

naturally discipline you to be one-pointed by the force of its attack—so be one-pointed first. At this time be determined, with all your forces, to be more aware of your inner spiritual companionship and protection; stand aware of your invincible godhood in the Christ within, then fear will recede and order will come in its place. But you must not be half awake mentally. Those who win do not deviate; and so your energies at this life-creating moment must be used to keep yourself undisturbed in God's power. Do not let the moments go by you unlighted.

You sometimes wonder why certain things are given you to bear; do not, for it is a waste of time. Put your desire, your pent-up feeling, into the pure desire of being with him, and watch during the day the extraordinary waste of thinking that unmans and weakens. It is the discipline of one's thoughts that matters, the turning inward and resting in that deep center where all is still and safe and sure. Great is the companionship and the peace of so doing, and be sure you know you are doing your best.

Receive in quiet the assurance of your protection.

The flowing out of God always demands a flowing back.

                                        Ruysbroeck

Wherefore when you find yourself in this confidence with our Lord, stay there without moving yourself to make sensible acts, either of the understanding or of the will; for this simple love of confidence and this rest of the spirit . . . contains by excellence all that you go hither and thither to satisfy your taste. It is better to rest here than to watch elsewhere.

                            St. Francis de Sales, 1567-1622

Contemplation is a perception of God or of divine things; simple, free, penetrating, certain, proceeding from love and tending to Love.

Louis Lallemant, 1587-1635

∽

TODAY WE WILL HAVE A PRIMER TALK. WHAT IS CONFUSING to you I imagine is that you have not quite understood what takes place when you place a new thought, a sun-thought, in the galaxy which makes your identity, especially such powerful ones as you have been given. You do not take, as it were, a new concept in your hands, place it in the midst of the familiar galaxy and expect a sudden radiance, an immediate change, although I do not forget that instant revelation and realization have come to some of the great ones who have walked this way. No, like all good things this work begins humbly. It is like planting a seed that grows and grows for a time in the dark. Ideas that have been given you in these communions are in movement and as they grow larger and larger they push out into oblivion the older ideas which were foolish and out of proportion. This is difficult to put into words, but it may help you not to be too introspective.

When you meditate or abide in your quiet times of communion, you do not charge in and do something, like saying, "I will now be good and move mountains by my act of faith." No, you water your garden, knowing that these ideas are growing into a heavenly garden; the indwelling spirit doeth the work, not you; you merely water it. Do you not see the comfort there is in that? I can tell you in primer language that a very gentle, calm, unemotional selfless and patient attitude toward your spiritual growth is essential—such as all old gardeners know. They know that patience, hoeing, watering and a certain order, a quiet rhythm, bring to birth a heavenly beauty.

How to do this in your particular, demanding, galloping tempo is difficult; but I will, in primer language, give you suggestions. In the morning I sit down to my breakfast and I eat my food; this is a voluntary action. I do not think about what is happening, but strength is being given me, life is being sustained, a great miracle has taken place. In the same way your words and thoughts are transmuted, for the food you give your mind also becomes flesh as well as part of your identity as an individual. Your part is your acceptance or rejection, and what you accept becomes a growth of some kind in your garden. But let us go further and see how we can use these everyday things to help us to greater awareness of the abiding Presence in our lives, to help us to dominion over our earth-consciousness. Let us not only recognize that we find an analogy in our earthly life, but let us use each thing that comes as a reminder.

In this rebirth into self-conscious realization of your godhood, take the homely common simple actions and make them follow the same law on a higher plane. I eat and drink in remembrance of him eternally alive in me; it is a profound communion and a great practical help. As you eat the bread of life spiritually with the bread materially, your inspiration will strengthen you for the day. As I have told you, this is a primer lesson, for what is needful for you is to keep in contact with the Spirit, to make the habit of doing so. And you yourselves will change by forming the habit of tenderness toward common things, the habit of communing and bringing down into everyday actions the heavenly grace. Everything you touch, feeling the warmth of an open fire, is an outward and visible witness of the spiritual law. Bathe in water as you would in spirit. Water is the source of life, it is a spiritual symbol. Let the shock of it on your flesh be a reminder of your contact with the invisible faith within you. Use your imaginations and be like that humble friar, Brother Lawrence, or the great artists of all time, who took the humble simple things close to them and transfigured them and themselves. For spiritual awakening allies you to the great poets and artists. Such is the wonder and the grandeur of the spirit, its transforming and glamorous beauty.

Gradually these ideas, these thoughts that have entered through your spiritual heart will grow as involuntarily as the food you eat is taken care of without effort, and the inner you will manifest so gently that as you go into the world your feet will be led to walk beside the watered garden of your own making. Illumine the common things and you will fill your skies with stars. Go, seeking goodness and you will find it; seeking beauty and it will be upon your face. Thus will you walk the glorious way, using the common elements of daily life as rods and staffs. Nothing is too small for your consideration and for your use.

There—I have spoken for children tonight in this primer. Contact, was my text. "Do this in remembrance of me." Do all things in remembrance of him—*remember your way out!*

I will add a postscript, for children in eagerness sometimes run too far ahead. Do not feel yourself a slave to this idea, for the mind is so constructed that if you drive it with spur and bridle it will balk. Remember always with joy and never with strain or boredom, for love only can find the way.

> *And look that nothing remain in thy working mind*
> *but a naked intent stretching unto God,—not clothed*
> *in any special thought of God in himself or any of his*
> *works, but only that He is as He is. . . . Forsake good*
> *thoughts as well as evil thoughts. He asks no help but*
> *only thyself. He will thou do but look upon Him*
> *and let him alone.*
>
> The Cloud of Unknowing, 14th Century

Man is no star, but a quick coal
    Of mortal fire;
Who blows it not, nor doth control
    A faint desire
Lets his own ashes choke his soul.

. . .

Life is a business, not good cheer;
    Ever in wars.
The sun still shineth there or here,
    Whereas the stars
Watch an advantage to appear.

. . .

Oh that I were an orange-tree
    That busy plant!
Then should I ever laden be,
    And never want
Some fruit for Him who dressed me.

George Herbert, 1593-1632

SINCE THE BEGINNING IT HAS ALWAYS BEEN A QUESTION OF minus or plus, spiritual or material, light or darkness. Everyone who has made a stand and called upon the unseen to reveal itself goes through the backing and filling on the borderline between the two. For every act of faith there is a challenging fear. The outer you is naturally dismayed by the turmoil, and we are here to bear witness that like the steady captain on the bridge in the storm, you must face it and be confident in the unseen. Your growing intelligence makes you realize that you cannot afford to let go and be swept into chaos. You *can* hold your universe together. There is an ebb and flow of hope and disappointment; courage followed by fear and weariness. But be of good cheer for your very realization and intent at this moment is a reward.

I have often told you that the running of the race is more important than the race. Many have had to run it over hot sands and have brought the spirit of Christ down to make a stream of living water in a wilderness. Take the whole dare and yield to faith; that is all that lifts a man out of the herd. Say, "Christ is my refuge, my comforter, the supplier of my needs. He changes water into wine, he gives me my daily bread and lifts my spirit with his own." Believe that you can translate your godhood, your love of God, through Christ into a daily miracle.

It is hard to smile with happy faith, I know, when the heart is being clutched at and terror is a dark sky for scenery. But at least you have this evidence, that you turned to your Father in time, and the very turning to him for strength gives strength. That is an act of God.

> *Be still and cool in thy own mind and spirit from thy own thoughts, and then thou wilt feel the principle of God to turn thy mind to the Lord from whom cometh life; whereby thou mayest receive the strength and power to allay all storms and tempests.*
>
> *The Diary of George Fox;*
> From the record of a letter to Cromwell's daughter

> *I said to heaven in the beginning when there was no night, that there must be purity of thought.*

> *One may heal with holiness, one may heal with the law, one may heal with the knife, one may heal with herbs, one may heal with the Holy Words; amongst all remedies this one is the healing one that heals with the Holy Word.*
>
> *Zoroastrian Scriptures*

YES IT IS TRUE; THE OUTER YOU HEARS AS THROUGH A VEIL, but the inner you translates the delicate suggestions of serene timeless peace, understands the message of the Word whenever it is spoken. That is why we are sometimes confused and mistaken in a personality which at once understands the message in all its fullness. We begin to hear more clearly when our desires are purified. It has been said that the sincerity of our faith is proved by our habits of response; this applies also to our desires, those quick almost involuntary desires that reach out before thought clears in the mind. For this reason beware of heavy habits, for where a habit is fastened upon you it is a sign of thickness; instead, realize that every moment has power within it and that with every heartbeat, with every breath you can be lifted out of the prison of a negative personality through co-operation with the indwelling Spirit. Be not dismayed; know that your Redeemer liveth and that you can know God. See him in everything; and you do not have to make an effort to see him for he is with you in every act and you are hearing him when you make the wise choice in times of decisions. Remember, too, that in every second of the day you are making decisions—not upon what you shall do but *what you shall think*, and that is what matters. Every instant the mind is accepting or rejecting, going forward or back, up or down. For this reason we are trying to help you practice the presence of God and this must not be done as a pleasant and comforting ritual to be used only when you are under stress; it the gift of the spirit to be realized with joy, to be known as a renewing power, to be understood as our only life, for through it man comes into his godhood. It is the pathway for the spiritual evolution of the race—and Jesus taught no other. You have a gigantic task; do not belittle it.

Do not too much talk at or about great truths instead of realizing your divine gifts. How easily we blame circumstances, how frequently we hear (with profound sympathy from our own travail) the tragic cry, "Why, oh why?" And yet how seldom do we hear within ourselves those words which hold so explicitly the condition of free will, "*Because* he hath set his heart upon me I will deliver him"; "*if* ye abide in me and my words abide in you ye shall ask what ye will and it will be done unto you"; "he that abideth in me and I in him, the same bringeth forth much fruit"; and "in that day shall this song be sung . . . thou wilt keep him in perfect peace whose mind is stayed on thee."

I will finish now with a quotation from one of long ago; "For our Lord shall be in thy side ready and nigh to thine help, and He shall keep thy foot (that is the ascending of thy love by which thou goest to God) so that thou shalt not be taken by subtlety nor guile of thine enemies—the world and the flesh. Lo! friend, thus shall our Lord and our Love, mightily, wisely and goodly succor, keep and defend all those that for lovely trust that they feel in Him will utterly forsake the keeping of themselves."

He brought light out of darkness, not out of a lesser light; he can bring thy summer out of winter, though thou have no spring; though in the ways of fortune or understanding or conscience, thou have been benighted till now, wintered and frozen, clouded and eclipsed, damped and benumbed, smothered and stupified till now, now God comes to thee, not as in the dawning of the day, not as in the bud of the spring, but as the sun at noon.

John Donne, 1573-1631

ᴖ

THE CONFUSING ASPECT OF YOUR PROGRESSION IS OFTEN DUE to the fact that your conception of how events should be shaped is never fully realized your way; they are largely influenced by your emotional states and your thoughts. It is hard for you to see this, being in the midst of details which are insistent and pressure which is immediate. As we have said before, use the little things in your daily life as reminders; if a bell rings, a clock strikes the hour, stop for a moment and say, "Where am I at this moment? Am I in a state of ignorance, of tension, in a heavy place? Or am I reaching upward, purifying my whole nature through my listening spirit so that the burdens of obstruction will not be in my path? For that is how to melt your way through your difficulties, it is the way of peace and not the way of war. Much is said today of the horror of war between nations, but I tell you that the private wars in the darkness of the human consciousness are no less violent and alarming, and they eventually become manifest in injury to oneself as well as to others. It is time to face this, and it is why we tell you over and over to keep gentle within, to "leave all quietly to God" and to awake to your godhood and to be Godlike, Christlike in your feeling toward your fellow men. The ungentle way is war, and is never victory. Remember that evil is that which is out of balance, and he that is out of balance cannot achieve, as you desire to achieve. Keep your balance by not plunging into thoughts of terror, of suspicion and criticism, for he cannot walk in the company of such thoughts. You have at last reached the place where you sense a sustaining love, a protecting spirit; be more and more confident that the work of the Father is always done within first, and keep your divine balance so that when events come to trouble you, you will not be weak and your thoughts scattered and uncontrolled. Be encouraged by the thought that there is an involuntary life going on within you, a healing is taking place, a freeing from dark emotions because you have asked to go the divine way. Let in the light to shine upon your anxieties, to shine upon each problem and be divinely expectant always.

One of you says, "I was swept into the outer circle, thoughts of resentment and forboding, of pride and fear pulled me down." Nay, do not be too much hurt. Step back, sit down quietly and a table will be set before thee in the presence of those enemies. Listen, listen for your very life! Learn this utter stillness so that he can come in times like these; even lay aside the remembrance of these thoughts and rest with your whole mind and soul on the surety of the Shepherd's guiding hand; follow happily through the valley of shadows; follow with full trust, bless each moment and purify it. Challenge each concept, remove the dross before accepting, and in this state of holy awareness time will dissolve, pressure will be lifted, doubt released and ye shall be free indeed. Go with a tender step, giving unto others what has been given to you.

The order of the world is no accident. There is nothing actual which could be actual without some measure of order. The religious insight is the grasp of this truth: That the order of the world, the depth of reality of the world, . . . the beauty of the world, the zest of life, and the mastery of evil, are all bound together—not accidentally, but by reason of this truth; that the universe exhibits a creativity with infinite freedom, and a realm of forms with infinite possibilities: but that this creativity and these forms are together impotent to achieve actuality apart from the ideal harmony, which is God.

Alfred Lord Whitehead, 1861——

*I beseech thee for to draw us up . . . to the height of
thy dark inspired speakings where all things of divin-
ity be covered and hid under the sovereign-shining
darkness of wisest silence.*

Part of the Prayer attributed to St. Denis,
circa 13th Century

∽

MAKE THE HABIT OF WORSHIP IN EVERY ACT OF YOUR DAILY
life; and by that I do not mean a solemn duty but
rather an overtone of feeling, a high clear note which you
sound at the beginning of each day and which you can half
consciously hold while occupied with the varying and often
humdrum scales of your many activities. There is no other exercise that will so control the subconscious emotional states
which can quickly precipitate you into discord and violence.
Worship, and allow no alarm to magnify itself. Worship is a
giving out of love to the holy Spirit, to God, to Christ, our
eternal companion, and with it comes a warming sense of companionship; it is, as one has said, "a witness to His glory." Let
the inner you "banish all that disturbs; let the body which
envelops it be still, and all the frettings of the body and all
that surrounds it; let earth and sea and air be still, and heaven
itself. And then let the man think of the Spirit as streaming,
pouring, rushing and shining into him from all sides while he
stands quiet." This, my children, is worship.

All that is asked of you is to be childlike in your devotions
and illumination, in the highness of your thought. When
reality hardens the human spirit and there is a space of time
that is like a desert, and the memory of illumination is so
clouded by the daily life you cannot recall it to be an oasis in
the dry sand, which at the moment stretches to your horizon,

then, to use an old phrase, take yourself in hand, for as one says, "With thinking we may be beside ourselves in a sane sense. By a conscious effort of the mind we can stand aloof from actions and their consequences, and all things good or bad, go by us like a torrent." Then is the time to recall to your remembrance what you have received and to hold the lamp of vision high; this is the work of the inner you and it will never fail if you will make the effort.

You may have the experience of finding that the thoughts of your outer you will try to march over you like an army; but cling to your intent, release yourself from the sense of past and future in time, and receive. Let each moment come, strong, illumined, as cool as water to quench your thirst, breath to your nostrils in the heavy air, and health and peace to your body. Picture the spirit within you, to which you turn, as a calm inward flame; your quietly holding it is what is important. Meditation is discovering it, releasing it, acknowledging it in all the ways of your life. You are actually hung in space by pure thought; you are not a body corporeal; that is not the reality, that is the stumbling experiment. You are deathless, true, divinely breathing eternity as you go. So stay within and let all things without resolve. Have confidence; be patient with genius; burst into a light of patience!

Rest, then, in a divine suspension, bring the invisible into the visible; his is the only victory. Abide in him in the quiet of overtone feelings and remember that "he hath given me a being as wide as eternity."

> *When thou purposest thee to this work, lift up thy heart to Him with a stirring of love . . . and receive none other thought of God, for a naked intent directed unto Him without any other cause than himself, sufficeth wholly.*
>
> *The Cloud of Unknowing*, 14th Century

IN REPLY TO YOUR NEED I MUST SAY WHAT I HAVE ALREADY
said so often, that simplicity of approach is what you re-
quire at the moment; if you could only see, if you could only
hear, if you could only know how simple, how tender, how
radiant is the feeling of oneness with your indwelling Spirit!
I shall try and compare it to a very human experience. When
you were in love your imagination was held captive by the
one you loved and your whole tone was uplifted to that ob-
ject. Often the image of your beloved was more real than the
actual person, who was as unreal and as unseen as I am at this
moment as I write to you. I can only repeat that to receive
the sense of the love of the Spirit, to receive the divine wisdom
and knowledge, you must truly ponder and meditate and hold
the high image steady and true, as you so *involuntarily* held
that human image of your beloved.

It is true that you are at the place of your desire, that you
want this infinite peace and comfort in a troubled world, and
it is difficult, with the interests and alarms of the day to return to a quiet moment of communion like the one of this
moment, as you read; it is hard to conjure up in your mind
the quality of feeling your mind is now touching. But if you
were really in love you would not have to search for this feeling; that involuntary emotion would tone your whole day,
the trees would take on a richer hue, the skies clear, and even
the people in the street would seem endowed with nobility
because that emotion would of itself clasp and hold high the
very jewel of your heart's desire. The materialist knows this
and he would say that it is impossible to live in the tempo of
youth's first love, and yet I say to you that this is the way and
the truth and the life.

You will grow to love the beauty and the clarification of

the revelations that will come to you and you will learn gradually that this peace, calm knowledge and inspiration are part of the rebirth that has been the prophecy through the ages for all those who walk this path, the prophecy fulfilled through love. Is not this peace, is not this powerful knowledge, is not this love worth all that you can give?

And remember that the more tender, the more open, the gentler you can be in your quiet time of acceptance, of stillness, the greater will be the power pressed through your silences.

I would again bring to your remembrance that you can love your way out of all seeming frustration; by loving to be silent, by loving to tune the infinitely delicate instrument of your mind to its high purpose. I hear you say, "Oh, why does it not work?" It *has* worked in precisely the same measure of the loving you have put into it.

In quiet listen to the Spirit within you speak:

> My will in thee is joy not sorrow
> My will in thee is faith not fear
> My will in thee is awareness of My love for thee,
> Let My will within thee be done.

> *Truly it is Life that shines forth in all things!*
> *Vast, heavenly, of unthinkable form, it shines*
> *forth . . .*
> *It is farther than the far, yet near at hand,*
> *Set down in the secret place of the heart . . .*
> *Not by sight is it grasped, not even by speech,*
> *But by the peace of knowledge, one's nature*
> *purified—*
> *In that way, by meditating, one does behold Him*
> *who is without form.*
>
> **The Upanishads**

THE MYSTERY OF DEVELOPMENT REACHES SO FAR BACK IT IS difficult to explain and to understand; the blessed thing is that you have come into the realization of the spiritual adventure and that your intent is forward. Your body, too, will be freed from much heaviness; in the crystal clearness of your new world you will breathe in health. All that goes on within you, the multitude of things that beat and move, the pilgrimage of the blood to the heart, the refreshment of sleep and all the traffic and business of the corporeal self will be conducted with greater ease and lightness. The push of divine life, the celestial instinct that doth pierce thy worldly inertia—all is from the same source; it pushes through the reluctant outer self which would sit and wail and rub ashes in its hair.

Can you stand and think in perfect stillness that you are but the expression of the long thrust upward of an idea, casting off all weights, all heavy feelings in the realization of the upward flight? Cast off everything; be the forward part of the thrust, illumined, your light breaking forth from within. Such imagery will help you to realize the power within you, if in the same thought you are aware of the source of that Light. And remember that those who thrust upward are often dismayed by their errors. That is part of the high adventure, for those who win must not look to the right nor to the left; in great height do not look down. Do not curse yourself or bewail. There are many strange faces and subtle masks that present themselves to all upon this journey; there are the whisperers who bring the temptations of fear and doubt. Keep in the thrust and you shall be freed and given the strength and power for your journey. Rest on this and be comforted, for if you turn to look and listen you will fall into the descending spiral round and round descending, saying, "I am this, I am that, I should have done other things . . ." Nay, look straight before thee, for thou art one-pointed and all who come nigh thee shall be lifted also. This is for thee, my child; for thy mind, thy soul, thy body. Live in eternity, the ever-present.

In the idea of victory there is power; in the word "victory" there is also a sense of effort, but in this new way, *rest in the idea* of victory which is being won for you through your stand. Rest in the serenity, the clarity of your inspiration, knowing that you are being freed. Let go your outer you, keep in touch with the inner you which is quick, alive and at secret attention. There is no strain in this for it is the peace of perfect order and balance; step forth and stand in light; stand as on spiritual parade!

> *There are those who say, "I am not one of those extraordinary souls, I have no mystical gifts, I do not aspire to such things, I will keep the common way," and persuade themselves that that is the spirit of their vocation. To them I say, No; you haven't experienced these unions and heard these high calls to God and perhaps that is why it is so difficult to calm you when you are put out by some little thing, as when you are slighted. If you had a higher understanding of perfection and if you looked always to Him and found comfort in Him you might be admitted to these unions that make the heart so strong nothing can disturb it.*
>
> John Joseph Surin, 1600-1665

> *Were I asked why, seeing that so many people have undertaken the direct service to God, there are so few saints, I would answer that the chief reason is that they have given too big a place in life to indifferent things.*
>
> *Ibid.*

Only actions done in God bind the soul of a man.

The Upanishads

◡

TODAY I WANT TO SPEAK TO YOU ABOUT FAITH, AND A perfect faith; that beneficent, uplifting spirit. Let us symbolize it as a child in happy surroundings, protected and loved, going about its delightful affairs upon a bright day, attracted by gay flowers and friendly animals. It suddenly trips upon a stone and is cast upon its face, meeting hard reality. It is set upon its feet, washed and comforted; soon the pain leaves and happy things blot out the memory of pain. High spirits raise it to a state of excitement until it comes sharply upon ugliness, a dead animal, and terror enters its heart. I won't go on with this and how faith is forever challenged by malice, fear and disappointment from without and from within.

Now, the happy child in you is the supreme state and the task before you is to learn that the hurts and the disappointments are not for the child; they are to be overcome by the instinct for joy which is your heritage and the pearl of great price; the natural instinct for joy which is to become the joyful awareness of spiritual oneness with him and the realization of the power therefrom. Joy is the conquering element and that is why it is deceiving, for we have smothered our feeling of right to it with outworn traditions and false standards of duty. The smiling spirit of faith, childlike and trustful, denying *through the integrity of its trust* all evidence of despair, is the crowned king, Jesus the infant, the holy symbol of your complete freedom from the hurt of the stones, the flinty ground, the tragedy of death and the ills of mortality. Rediscover that Child within you, for when your "enemies shall come in like a flood" he will teach you "to lift up a standard against them."

If I think my source is diluted and muddied, my supply of water will not be clear. If I do not believe that the infinite Spirit is perfection, that it is unalloyed goodness and beauty, I shall not receive unmixed goodness and beauty. If I do not believe that the principle of proportion can give balance and order, I cannot use it to give me those results.

If I "ask" believing that something besides joy can come from the Giver, I shall not receive pure joy. If when I "knock" I am doubtful of him who stands the other side of the door, I shall not find my Friend. If I am suspicious of his gifts they will not be the gifts I need.

If I hold doubt between me and faith, I shall not be free from the results of fear.

But if I open to receive, with perfect faith that only goodness can come from Goodness, confident as a child that I shall be given what I most grievously need, then, and then only, my cup runneth over.

There is within us a power that could lift the world out of its ignorance and misery if we only knew how to use it, if we would seek and find. When you meditate open not only your listening mind, but the other door of your mind as well, so that the spirit streams out as fast as it comes in. Store nothing. . . . A tree grows not by the pulling of the sun only, but by the richness of the soil. . . . Go into the calm and luminous silence to renew, but stay in the soil of your life. No, there is nothing to fear. Do not waste time wishing for peace; there is no peace in a world, there is only peace in one's own soul. Get more fearless peace into your souls and then you will be some good!

Letter from J. P. M.

YOU ARE BEGINNING TO COMPREHEND THE VITALITY OF YOUR thoughts; how they will race and clash and confuse and tire the orderly rhythm of one's living, day and night. Thoughts can seize and fasten onto the consciousness. Now take boldly the role of commander; calm these unruly soldiers in your company by commands, by great words of spiritual intent. As you were warned, do not go down with the stream, remain at the source, the source within you. Be the eternal spring. This indeed is a task for a man, but here is the victory won. Perhaps words like these will help you; say, to yourself, "I am a messenger. I will not waste my life on the letter, but I will seek the Spirit and hold myself at the source. I will obey the word; I will not be delayed in the treadmill of human, negative thought. I will escape all useless mental anxiety. Lord, here I stand, obeying thy words, knowing that in obeying the divine command my burden will be lifted." Lean, lean therefore on thy strong reassuring inner self, realizing that in obedience God's will is done to the end of time. Nothing is too small, nothing too large. "Say not lo, here! nor lo, there!" Nor be dragged here and there and about, for indeed the kingdom of all peace and power is within you. Stay—and advance!

Try dissolving your universe, as you have been told before, into spiritual and mental concepts; consider yourself a feeling that has been led about by the events of your time. Character is, in its last analysis, a collection of feelings. A good man is a trust-feeling. If you dissolve all people to thought and examine your own thought as you carry it about you will see with greater clarity how destructive it is to be a Fear. If you are a Fear, you at once become a vortex which attracts to you currents of obstacles and blockings. But if you are a Confidence going though the unseen, as your true world really is, if you are a spirit of courage, calm and loving, you act like a sun on all about you and grateful faces will turn to you as you touch the creative impulse everywhere. It is as simple as this. Guard yourself from states and when you find yourself sinking into one and you stand before the walls of your Jericho, blow your silver bugle and your clear note of prayer will be heard. Great and good forces are your companions; you do not walk alone, Christ is in your heart.

How little are the blind men; come within that your eyes may be opened and you may see. Stretch your identity, widen your faith, lift your mind and keep out all material and entangling thoughts—let them dissolve and fall like sediment. *Take* no thought; *be* thought; "have the mind of Christ."

> *It is good to tame the mind, which is often difficult to hold in and flighty, rushing wherever it listeth; a disciplined mind brings happiness.*
>
> *Buddhist Scriptures*

∽

WHEN YOU ARE IN COMMUNION YOU ARE IN THE PIVOTAL place, in the center where your safety lies; you are in balance, for this is the plumb bob that does not sway in the midst of alternating violence and peace. It keepeth all in quietness, steady and true. When you are here you are in the center of the storm; keep to this point, timeless, immortal and omniscient. This is too transcendent for you to grasp except at fleeting moments like this, but be faithful in intent and all you need will be revealed to you.

There are simple exercises that may help you; sometimes lie still in silence when you are tired and feel the earth turning under you, the universe of stars above and below, held together by this serene force that is within yourself. Lie there and receive in silence, and *let* the light shine through every cell of your flesh and bones and say "Thy kingdom come, Thy will be done in earth as it is in heaven." Again, think of your heart as the center of the universe and let it say "Light!" with every heartbeat; or when you find yourself walking, as it were, to your destruction, come to a halt and say these words, "I am aware of thee, that thou are beside me," and then walk with him wherever you go.

These are but exercises, but they can be important. Put all your faith in this secret-holding companionship and you will be astonished. It is becoming as a child.

Yes, this is a time to be aware of this great birth, baneful though it be. Hold yourselves to Yourselves; be spiritually tough, indeed be holy. No compromise; and do not keep this as a sort of sanctimonious concept to turn to vaguely. Take the dare and converse with God. Ask him simply and bring him into your life and you will then not blank out so often. Once there was an ancient king who, upon the day of his coronation felt that all his hopes had come to fulfillment, for he was crowned after many years of waiting, king of a great realm. As he sat in the cathedral in his vestments, his orb and scepter in his hands, his crown upon his head, he saw a fault in the uniform one of his generals was wearing and his mind was taken to that and he forgot that he was at the great moment of his life and the moment passed him by.

Try not to let these ephemeral, impinging, daily pinpricks steal away your immortality, which you can begin to know now, for this is your great moment, now . . . now . . . now. Now is the time of thy salvation, and salvation means safe return. Arise and shine for thy light has come.

Listen, or thy tongue will keep thee deaf.

American Indian

*The Disciple said to his Master: Sir, how may I come
to the spiritual life so that I may know God and hear
Him speak?*
*The Master answered: Son, when thou canst throw
thyself into that where no creature dwelleth, though
it be but for a moment, then thou hearest what God
speaketh.*
*Disciple: Is that where no creature dwelleth near at
hand or is it afar off?*
*Master: It is in thee. . . . If thou dost once every
hour throw thyself by faith beyond all creatures, beyond and above all sensual perception . . . yea above
discourse and reasoning, into the abyssal mercy of
God, then thou shalt receive power from above to
rule over death and sin.*

Jacob Boehme, 1575-1624

∽

THE TIME HAS COME TO LIFT THE VERY SPIRIT OF YOU INTO
the current of faith; it is indeed a current, a mighty, creative, creating recreating revivifying mood which, when
reached, will set free an active joyous inspiration beyond your
conception. You cannot keep the Spirit disincarnate if you
abide in it. This power has touched the great ones of the
earth; it has changed the tide of battle, for it is inward
strength; it is courage, it has a hundred names. Keep in the
current of faith, the tone of faith, for it is the tone of morale.
Create the atmosphere of achievement, creative expectancy.
Forbid all negative impatience, for in this mood is high hope
and assuring trust. It is an uplifting form of communion free
from the heat, noise and confusion of human personality. It
is augustly impersonal; it is divine order, it is perfect balance
and can only be reached by the discipline of appetites—appe-

tites for anger and criticism, resentment and self-justification. You can be led far afield by angry strangers and your own desire to present your outer personality favorably. It is the old enemy, the egotist; from selflessness within to sudden self without is a sharp change! Faces, voices, chameleonlike personalities confuse and alter your whole scale of values abruptly in the outside world. The mind can trip and sprawl when caught by the snatching, insistent difficulties of daily living. There is a zero hour for all who hold high their thought, their vision—waiting to meet the temptation of fear with courage. But as we have told you many times, courage is your only safety. Practice the little tests as you would practice putting into use any useful knowledge, and the more you do this the more are you saved "ordeals by fire," for you acquire a strength which will not fail, through the sense of your daily companionship with him who walks with you, whose strength you use, whose power is yours for the asking, whose mightiness is illumination and whose gentleness can make you great.

I am thy holy Spirit of inspiration within thee, I am thy power to fulfill it.

Anonymous

ᔪ

W HEN TRAPPED BY WALLS OF DISAPPOINTMENT AND TEMPTED to panic by disordered thinking, calmness is the only solution for men; for the acts of Providence are so hidden it is hard to understand how delicate are the influences emanating from you, from your minds. There are great changes that come about in the darkest hours when there is no hope and the encircling gloom is terrifying to the heart, and it is difficult for the human to understand the power at that moment. Calmness in the midst of chaos, serenity in the midst of feverish activity is the secret that all commanders must know—

the secret revealed in crises, that the soul that is calm with controlled emotion is performing an act of faith; the easier you play the game of fortitude the more relaxed you become to each challenge of impatience, the more you control your destiny. To do this you must remember your way back into the very center of your being, to that eternal fountain of refreshment within. Otherwise you block, frustrate and delay, for a frantic spirit is a stupid one. It is a hard lesson when it should be the softest. Let us consider it for a moment; you believe that you are sons of God, you hold the vision of your godhood. The human, bewildered, tired, impatient self can only glimpse this in moments far apart, as you call time. You can only reach God in stillness, in calmness. What is a week, a month in this august destiny? Play the part nobly and refuse this frantic littleness; stand and wait. Harassed and shaken I knew all those relentless bedfellows. Be comforted, be comforted and learn that destinies are controlled by the delicacy of your calmness within, by your turning to the divine companion who never leaves nor forsakes thee. I would recall to you your first thoughts when it was told to you that through contemplative stillness you would be able to reach your God, that through this silence your inward and secret light would be revealed to you. So now, in times like this, I bring you this remembrance; it is the same, it is the good news, the everpresent revelation. You cannot and will not reach what you desire through emotional explosions; you know this—now obey. Come where the eternal Spirit, Love itself, untangles, loosens and pulls away from you all that binds, for it unshackles these imprisoning chains, these iron bands of thought and silences the gongs of fear and dismay.

In your outer active life translate humble things into divine things; use this actual outside living as a way to God. Take the serene and timeless peace of a great mountain, feel its vast serenity when you write a letter or stamp an envelope or

perform what seems to you very unimportant labors. Bring
the divine power into actual life and beautify it.

So peace be unto your hearts and great stillness and calm.
Seek this creative peace within; here there is no struggle. Here
are beauty and truth and protection and joy in abundance.
Here is order; and here, locked away, is the divine plan. When
you dissolve and become still, holy in that oneness with the
infinite holiness, the divine plan cometh to pass and you are
free. You are challenged out there; in here the challenge is
defeated. Seek and worship the Father.

> *You are a distinct portion of the essence of God; and
> contain part of him in yourself. Why, then, are you
> ignorant of your noble birth? Why do you not con-
> sider whence you came? Why do you not remember,
> when you are eating, who you are who eat; and
> whom you feed? Do you not know that it is the Di-
> vine you feed; the Divine you exercise? You carry a
> God about with you, poor wretch, and know nothing
> of it.*
>
> Epictetus, A.D. 50

IT IS A GOOD THING TO PLACE SENTINELS AROUND YOUR MIND,
for when it is unguarded it slips away and emotions rush
the gate and take command. There is nothing wrong with
the human race except destructive emotions. You cannot be
attacked except through the strength or weakness of emotional
ups and downs. This in itself sounds fearful and if we walk
the common road it is fearful indeed. The secret is to lean
on no one but your inner self, through which you touch the
tenderness and the power of the almighty Spirit.

You know that you have been protected from many things
and old sores have been healed. For the future the great thing

is not to accept a destiny which appears dark before you, thus making it real and inevitable; but rather step aside lightly and go your way, laughing. Do not accept! Step aside and bring down light into your human darkness. It may be a delicate thing to do with so faint a result as only changing a mood from a conviction of hopelessness to one of doubt; a negative victory, to be sure, but you will have risen from minus to zero, at least. This is the way to heal the constant ache and recurring fear, and "stepping aside" is taking the ache within and melting it by your receptive awareness of the all-suffusing peace that abides there.

When you turn within release your imagination from ordinary concepts; let it take wing in as many varying images of reassurance as will rise to comfort you; the mind will finally grasp the one you need at the moment and hold to it. Lift up thine eyes unto the hills and peace will come on healing wings and you shall walk by still waters. This is not "wish-fulfillment" any more than giving into images that bring temptation to succumb to fear; and the effects can be judged in the lives and characters of those who choose the two ways of life. "I have set before thee life and death, therefore choose life that thou mayest live."

When you close your eyes and turn to the silence of the divine darkness you will have a sense of spaciousness without boundary, the timelessness of the joyous instant and the light of a new day.

Meditation is the clarifier of a beclouded mind.
                                        The Tibetan Doctrine

 ∽

THE THING EXPECTED OF YOU, THROUGH YOUR FINAL realization of all that has been told you, is to use your imagination so that you will not allow any separation from the Spirit by withdrawing, as it were, into forgetfulness. And if I must be literal that does not mean that you are to *think* of nothing else; it is an attitude of mind, or as someone has said, "an *altitude* of mind." Bring everything up to the high quality of the Spirit, do not take thoughts and problems down into the gloom of materialism nor of negative and despairing solutions. You have your communions, you receive the revelation that comes from them, you begin to sense the Presence, and then you are swept into forgetfulness. It is as if an angel came down and put on a garment, and the garment became illumined, went forth, took life and breathed; and then when the angel left, the garment collapsed into a shapeless thing. So it is in this way of life. But if you say, "I have no life except *with* the Spirit within me," you wear the garment through the sordid traffic of the world. And if it is unseen, that does not matter to you.

Forgetting this Life within is one of the problems we all face, and by certain self-disciplines we are helped to the greater awareness of the divine companionship.

We all know how the senses are dulled by great indulgence in the appetites that each one has, but what you do not quite understand yet is that refinement of perception comes from having dominion over them; you can release power within yourselves by sometimes overcoming a physical desire, by transmuting a mental greed of prejudice and criticism (the intense enjoyment of them) into a rushing awareness of wisdom, peace and justice through the realization of the presence of God. This is obedience; an obedience that is left with you to decide upon. There is a tonic value in your mastery which should give you an exhilaration, as a fine sport puts your body under your control and gives you the satisfaction of co-ordination.

Give over the indulgence of vain imaginings, melancholy, defeatism, a daily sense of martyrdom because of a situation in which you find yourselves. Make a spiritual constitution and live up to it, for it takes greater effort to release ourselves from these negative human emotions, which we say we hate, than to stand purified, cleansed and freed from these great delayers. You delay yourselves.

This is not spoken in censure; it is really an appeal to your intelligence. It is dangerous to slip back into the false ease-ment of emotional despondency, apprehension and fear. As you cleanse the body from fatty degeneracy you will realize that the fatty consciousness must go also. That is part of your spiritual constitution. And you can cleanse the body and cleanse the mind by the bright discipline of entertaining light.

Be careful not to think of this as effort. Obey the law; make up your mind. *Make up your mind* . . . ask and it shall be done unto you.

These are but suggestions; ponder on them for the love of Christ within; he is here in your flesh; he sustains, comforts and protects you. He abides with you, is merry with you, he is your friend. He is in dull people and in light people. He is beauty, he is your breath, and your encourager. So when you walk, wherever you go say, "Thou art here. I am not alone!"

As soon as a man turneth himself in spirit, and with his whole heart and mind entereth into the mind of God which is above time, all that ever he hath lost is restored in a moment. And if a man were to do thus a thousand times a day, each time a fresh and real union would take place; and in this sweet and divine work standeth the truest and fullest union that may be in this present time. For he who hath attained thereto, asketh nothing further, for he hath found the Kingdom of Heaven and Eternal Life on earth.

Theologia Germanica, 1497

EVERYONE HAS A CHOICE WHEN HE COMES TO THE crossroads where two ways lie; one concerns itself too much with this world; the other will hold your world together through the companionship of the Spirit. To be too much of this world is to waste time with possibilities and terrors. Also dwelling upon the angers and the hates leads to sorrow and sad events. The other road, the seeking of the Spirit in the kingdom within, will help to save the world and bring it to safe haven. This is your duty, this is your sacrifice, for your obedience is part of the leaven that will lift your country to great heights. But this is a discipline that you must take on personally, each for himself, for on either road you cannot escape discipline; *you will either be disciplined by events or you will make your own discipline.* Therefore make your own discipline and so contribute to great events. Be emotionally strong and firm, spiritually strong as steel, but controlled so that you can bend to shocks and not be uprooted by panics.

All that matters is your response to challenging events. If you are left alone to the inflowing and outflowing of human emotional relationships and the onslaughts of their passing moods you will find that your responses are immediate, you are undefended and emotionally exposed, quick to take fire. The value of these communions and of your silences is that in them you are strengthened and given poise; you are lifted high above the flood and you are given something strong, serene and healing. This is what is meant by the great words, "of myself I can do nothing"; you discipline yourselves so that you may receive, and you turn to complete acceptance of the outpouring gift of the Spirit.

Do not spill your soul in response to negative alarms and emotion. Be satisfied that you have the key, the name of the Spirit. Go in peace and abide with him.

Except the Lord keep the city,
The watchman waketh but in vain. It is but lost
labour that ye haste to rise up early, and so late
take rest,
And eat the bread of carefulness:
For so he giveth his beloved sleep.

Psalm 127 [Version of Coverdale]

﹏

IN THIS DISSOLVING WORLD WHEN EVENTS ARE SO QUICKLY
followed by events, in confusion, with personalities emerging out of the crucible, great and lasting changes are taking place and you are naturally assailed through your sensitiveness by the insistent alarms and cold fears that people are subject to. It is a moment when I would like to review your adventure on this journey toward light. Few seem to grasp the true meaning of religion; to many it is a hope through formalized prayers and dogmas to achieve a state of comfort and protection. But this is seldom realized because they leave religion to the teachers. In your adventure toward freedom you have taken an active part in your own development; you have sought sincerely and honestly a working method by which you could live as a channel for the Holy Spirit to flow through for your healing and cleansing and as a way to bring it into the world. You have become aware of receiving comfort and the protection that faith gives, and you know that the core of you is an inward calm, that it is steady and not subject to change. In a sense you have built an ark so that in this flood of emotion, of terror and uncertainty, you are safe. And by that I mean when tempted to dismay and bewilderment by the steady onslaught of news, you can open the invisible door and melt into the steadfast, quiet and confident center of your being.

The old disciplines of the monastic orders were devised to remind the stubborn flesh that it must not come first; the angelus, matins and vespers and the wayside crosses help many to remember the Spirit within. Today, instead of the hair shirt, the cruelty upon the body of the race drives us to the need of awareness of him to ease our hearts and sustain us, and hard as it is to believe, when you, each in turn, come to your God alone, within, by so much is this holocaust diminished; there is no greater way to practice the love of God, the brotherhood of man, and the fellowship of the Holy Spirit. Within this center of infinite quiet and peace lies resolution to action that is born of love and wisdom. Whenever challenged by the horrors or irritations of human living, you know that through the mind you can touch all that is august, deathless beauty and immortality.

What do we desire above all, above all? Perfect peace of mind, integrity, order, the victory of goodness, honor, joy and eternal love, free from human sentimentality and emotionalism; the high, clean impersonal rightness. Well, all these are for your asking . . . not praying, for your accepting and realizing and wanting.

Go your way step by step. Now is the appointed time to do your part; and your part, as you know well, cannot be done with righteous and breathless rectitude, but by being receptive so that you can be used as a channel, which is part of being a temple of the Spirit. It is the antithesis of noise and dubious fame; be the silent ones, anointed, with rod and staff and the scallop shell of quiet and the promise of truth.

> *I have resolved . . . to run when I can, to go when*
> *I cannot run, and to creep where I cannot go. As to*
> *the main, I thank Him who loves me, I am fixed;*
> *my way is before me, my mind is beyond the River*
> *that has no bridge.*
>
> John Bunyan, 1628-1688

As WE HAVE TOLD YOU SO OFTEN BEFORE, IT IS VITALLY important that you do not let the violence of the world rule your minds so that you live entirely on the circumference of the circle of your lives. Many people would be impatient if you should tell them that creative action, action based upon spiritual premises, is born in complete stillness, the stillness the inventor and scientist know in the laboratory. Not necessarily the stillness which is merely noiselessness alone, but the intense quiet of drawing upon the source of inspiration. "Be quiet and let me think!" is the cry of the man hard-pressed in the material world; and, though he often does not know it, he is demanding something within himself to show him the way out. For you the way out can be found more easily, more surely. "Let me be quiet that I may *know* . . . Thee."

Man ordinarily goes no further than his own experience (and that includes the experience of the race) for help in an emergency. But those who go still further within themselves for the answer will find a timeless wisdom and inspiration to be translated into the human need of the moment. "Call upon me in time of need and I will answer thee!" is not just a comforting thought to be forgotten when you have to act quickly and wisely in a material world. It is the most practical thing you can do.

In this time of conflict do not yield too much to the temptation of living in the violence; fast and pray, fast in your minds from doubt and fear. And when you pray do not pray too much as suppliants, do not beseech for the great and holy Gift already given you. Learn to receive, to accept and to use It.

"O Christ, omniscient within me, give me knowledge, knowledge of thyself in relation to my living day by day. Give me thy Spirit of eternal life to live now, on the earth, in the elements, in the world. Feed my mind with thy living bread; quench my thirst for thee with living water from the well of Life!"

THOUGH YOU ARE MOVED BY THE MIGHT OF OCEANS, THE infinity of sand, the high ceiling of heaven and outward vastness awes you by its diminishing influence, though you see mountain ranges and forests, the night blue of the sky with stars and planets and worlds beyond, though you hear of remote frozen seas and desolate wastes—do not belittle yourself, for this spiritual concept within you is deathless and all-powerful, measureless. Therefore when you look through your eyes at immensities know that that which you hold within is more powerful. Hold to this knowledge and fill yourself with faith, for it is your shield. Though you see multitudes in conflict emotionally and racially, be sure you are not impressed with your own littleness and inadequacy; that is the stupidity which cometh through ignorance. The ignorant are awed by show, the wise are awed by what is not seen, by thought. Hold the concept which encompasses more universes than you are yet aware of and through the complete humility of self and your service of faith you will become as yeast in the sodden world of materialism. Though your personal lives seem constricted and humble, it does not matter.

Do I have to warn you at this point? I will quote a brother who lived centuries ago. ". . . for meekness is imperfect and perfect; first a true knowing of the frailty of man, a feeling of a man's self as he is. The other the awareness of the over-abundant love of God in himself, in beholding of which all nature quaketh, all wise men be fools and saints and angels be blind." This infinite power is only revealed by the denial of self in the true sense and the glorifying of the Light within. Wherever you are you can touch this secret spark which is like radium in that it gives off an eternal and deathless energy. The time will come when you will have little to do with it because it will become more and more involuntary through your desire and need and love; it will gradually consume the outer you; it will cleanse you of your appetites for they will be uncomfortable in the presence of this radiance, and the false and ignorant will be healed away.

Use this indwelling spirit! How many pray to it and then go about their affairs under tension, taking upon themselves the burden from which they have asked to be freed, not trusting the God to whom they have prayed! In the *realizing oneness* with the Spirit do you find your working godhood; the beauty descending and ascending is your freedom. God moves in you now, through limitless space. Cast off your mooring from the land of fear and doubt, leave the prisons of despair and melancholy and set sail on a guided journey where the stars are in their appointed places and the voyage is true and beautiful and safe.

> Be active in silence
> Strong in peace
> Keep thy strength in gentleness
> Rest with the song of wings about thee
> Fill the inner reaches with love
> Bathe in Spirit
> For It is sweetness to thy bones flesh and health.
> Keep in this holy estate and listening—*obey!*

ℒ

THE CHEMISTRY OF YOUR BODY, AFFECTED AS IT IS BY emotional states, is very delicate, very sensitive; it is true in the strongest men. You are subject to thousands of influences; of some you are completely unaware; and if you could see to what some people react you would be astonished. Climate, fears most childlike, changes in temperature, old resentments, fear of cats, rainy days, depressing influences

from strangers, noises and even smells are constantly affecting
your bodily health; not to mention maladjustments. The
greatest thing to help you is the habit of being in the presence
of God. Your wish is for it, but as someone has said, *the proof
of a desire is found in the habit of response.* When this great
habit becomes more secure you will find an orderly faith is a
controlling, rejuvenating rightness, and your weak, defenseless,
awkward, too solid body will at last know what it means to
find fulfillment in the highest health. Oh, fill yourself with
light! Try every kind of way not to slide off the beautiful
smooth path where, if you could but stay, are no aches or
unease or sadness or pain or tiredness. Yes, you will find a
health more wonderful than any athlete's, for it will be a
vibrating faith. But *you* must do it. Be alert, industrious in
the habit of being in his presence. The fight is inch by inch,
never swerving. Learn that by these thorny struggles to keep
what you get and be strong in the holding of it, you will be
saved from having to go back to learn your lesson all over
again. All that is asked of you is to be gloriously happy and
it seems such a painful process! Watch every idle word, for
you will find joy in this wonderful game.

It is true the successes seem frail and delicate but they are
stronger than you can have any conception of, for because of
your intent you are being filled with healing, vitalizing, sustaining truth and eternal love; it is all on so grand a scale. You
will astonish yourself, and if you can see the simplicity of this
—the victory is yours.

Delay, delay—stop it now! Watch your every response and
thought and bring to yourself a day, a fraction of a day, when
you have kept his presence in your heart and your heart in
his presence; for this is the good news of which the prophets
spoke, this is what it is all about. This is what they meant
when they said "Rejoice!" for there is very little from which
we cannot be defended, and there is much that we can over-

come magnificently by learning not to sink down into darkness as the result of not being awake and alert.

Here he is—now. But man hates to think. He hates the effort of thinking, he is always seeking escape in the senses, in anything to get away from that which will make him free. Take the dare—for this is no foolish thing. Snatch moments, invent reminders, until this divine habit becomes constant. It is really as if you were in a place which is overcrowded, like a tenement street, and dark, and you knew a secret door that opened into a garden where there was quiet and everything had a friendly feeling; even the flowers and leaves turned toward you and the sky was aglow with infinite refreshment, that feeling of complete renewal of your tired mind, your weary flesh, and your clogged spirit. Walk as you would enjoying a rose garden, hear the fountains of goodness and the birds of joy singing.

There; that is a clumsy idea of what you will find when you slip through that door into his presence, but the mind of man is so constituted that he has to be told and retold and reminded that there *is* a door all the time, every hour of the twenty-four.

> I am the way, the truth and the life.
> Come unto me all ye who are heavy laden.
> Seek and ye shall find.
> My peace I give unto you.

Finally, be not afflicted nor discouraged to see thyself faint hearted; He returns to quiet thee, that still He may stir thee; because this divine Lord will be alone with thee . . . that thou mayest look for silence in tumult, solitude in company, light in darkness, forgetfulness in pressures, vigour in despondency, courage in fear, resistance in temptation, peace in war, and quiet in tribulation.

Miguel de Molinos, 1640-1697

THE FRAIL LIFE WHICH IS YOURS SETS FORTH UPON ITS journey weak and helpless, passing through storms and changes, strange unlockings unknown to your consciousness. Things hardly realized, influences beyond your conception make cross currents upon your destiny, upon this frail life which like a leaf blown high into the sky crosses mountains and valleys. In your day and times this life seems meaningless, terrifying and full of suffering, violent and easily brushed across the veil because of a thousand menacing dangers. The purpose of the inward struggles for integrity, to live, even to simply exist, stupifies the philosophers who like all the rest grope blindfolded through the first human stages, for the mystery is not revealed at once, but day by day, little by little and only to the seeker. I hear you say, "If I am in communion with the celestial influences, the Holy Spirit, why is my path not made smooth and why does it not bring about the instant destiny of my endeavor? Why is there this impenetrable wall between me and my aspiration and its fulfillment?"

Think. To fulfill any enterprise means that you meet other destinies also behind impenetrable walls, filled with emotions, desires, attributes different from your own. No wonder, therefore, that your little leaf is swirled high into the storms and revolts of other human destinies. This way is dark, the road hard and flinty and no one can free himself from the question Why? Why? The events of your times, stages in human personalities of those with whom you must march, add to your darkness and confusion. Under these circumstances of human living great can be the loneliness and the suffering. Life is awful indeed in its greater sense. But the hope and the wonder is that a change comes, a dawning, when you reach a place, when you step forward and choose wisely. You have acted upon your choice, you have stood your ground and have not weakened so that we can tell you to walk confidently carrying your dawning with you. Within you is the dawn, within you is the light, within you is the freedom, therefore with eye turned inward you are safe. Perhaps I speak to you behind many horizons but I can tell you that great is your hold upon the impenetrable secret which you have seized like children, not fully understanding, but with an instinct for this bright jewel which is all you really have. This dawn that you carry, clearing, clarifying, refreshing, is all that is needed for you. Live in it, abide in it, then let the leaves of your life blow free and high and you will find a true direction, a true control, ordered and inspired. "No harm shall come nigh thee" indeed, while you walk this Way, and the far-reaching of the Light you trust in is boundless and unknown to you as you sit here in this hour, in this century, in this universe.

Why you must not trouble yourselves with whys and wherefores is because it is a waste of time. You will be taught and learn as you go and as your need arises; and believe me, the fantastic heights of human knowledge are as nothing compared to the childlike instinct you have to go through all knowledge, all concepts to seize Light itself at its zenith. This is the known quantity. Seize and hold eternally to the highest and your feet will be guided through eternity, for it is your childlike faith that keeps your universe together.

When the question comes asking how it is possible that this little life as long as a breath or a sigh can be given power from the source of Life, reach up and hold the star, then things are revealed to you. But they are revealed in terms of character, they are revealed in voiceless feelings, in new strength, new vitalities, new freedoms, new shining glorious sinews until you are all light—*then* trust in It for when you are completely unafraid and clean in your faith, your life will be divinely inspired and you can step forth with a sure tread.

OVER A LONG PERIOD OF TIME YOU HAVE BEEN WARNED, prepared and fortified to meet violence and disorder; it is, therefore, like good soldiers of the Prince of Peace that you find yourselves on duty. Do not let a thought touched by cynicism penetrate your armor; do not wonder that a Prince of Peace should need an army, for "an armed man keepth his goods in peace" and the servants of Christ are defending the citadels of the Spirit which giveth Life and not death. The sword of the Spirit frees all men because its discipline is upon the man who bears it.

And now a high resolve is essential. Prepare yourselves for inward strength, a refuge within undisturbed, a realm august, the kingdom of heaven within your own consciousness, and let no destructive human emotion draw you from it.

Every individual has, within himself, a great part to play, and let no one think he is too small, too insignificant. For the power of the kingdom of heaven, when man makes way for it to pour through him as a channel in the stillness of disciplined and controlled emotion, cannot be measured, and there is nothing too great, nothing too small.

I cannot stress too much the responsibility of each one of you. Put God immediately before you and stand behind him, close, and you will be strengthened, comforted and instructed. Play this part all the day through, hold him up as a shield against the enemies within yourself and celebrate his birth each day within your own heart. In this way you serve your country and all men. Rest in the shelter of the silence where you can hear his word, and obey.

At the time of the festival of the Prince of Peace we are called upon in our daily human life to face violence. Our first defense is to turn to him with such rejoicing as we have never known before, for to rejoice is to worship, to acknowledge him our Saviour in a time of crisis. Hang the green garlands, light the tall candles, sing praise in an outpouring of thankfulness that he has shown us the way, the truth and the life of his glory. As was written centuries ago, "Come, come with me, O folk. Hasten to see Eternal Life in swaddling clothes!"

For this, "rejoice, I say unto you rejoice!"

Christmas, 1942

ॐ

IN EVERY WALK OF LIFE MAN FACES THE CURIOUS HURLY-burly of daily living which brings with it the wavering faith in the invisible realities, honor, integrity, principle. He often discards them as burdens in what seems to him a meaningless and futile world. It is the same with nations as with individuals when expediency replaces wisdom and the long view. In human occasions one's idea for oneself seems very pitiful; it is up and then down again, retrogression, self-betrayal and then hope and self-discipline, attack, retreat, sloughs, backwaters, opposing tides and gigantic fears, cruel realities.

No creative man in any endeavor escapes this sense of confusion and striving on the plane of material effort, whether he is a professional man, a businessman or an artist. But when he turns inward and leaves all this restfully to the serenity of deathless order he finds release and that the inner wisdom will rebuild his world out of chaos. There is no other way to this accomplishment. You cannot see the working for it as delicate as a butterfly's journey through a hurricane. It will light upon the most unexpected havens. It is true that the valley of the shadow is frightening and it is sometimes difficult to find him who says, "I am with you, I am thy rod and staff," but accept no negative whatever, particularly in the darkest moment, for you have been told that you are temples of the

Holy Spirit which abideth in you and never leaves you nor forsakes you. That trust in the dark brings light, not resignation which is often a negative, for man needs to believe that "when the enemy comes in like a flood the spirit of the Lord will lift up a standard against him." But *believe it!* In times of anxiety turn like a child to the simple instructions, knowing that "the Father within doeth the work" and that you can do nothing but rest in that assurance. Be high-careless, strong in faith, a spendthrift in love, keep a valiant heart, put on your crown and be a knight indeed!

Love conquereth all things.

AT THIS IMPORTANT TIME LET EACH ONE OF YOU BEGIN HIS day by listening. You will be told in answer to your need, and yet the voice is so impersonal in what it says you often brush it aside. Stay the hand, bend the ear and listen, for there is your success. Listen for your fresh inspiration, for even these communions can take on the same comforting, sedative quality as a ritual.

Each man at some time goes into the awful vault of himself; there alone he is silenced. It is here *you are before you became;* it is here you remain in the advance of inevitable progression. You may wonder how this thing you cannot see is yourself and you begin to be aware of how much of you is asleep. Also your whole record is here.

Not long ago we spoke of how "in the beginning was the Word." Can you see now that this inner place within you which has no boundary is also yourself? With the Word put into action you are Man made manifest. When at first you turn your attention to your own *withinness*, gradually through the dimness Light cometh in and you are, as it were, in a sea of twilight and you begin to know there is something that can be understood. Perhaps you are aware at this period of fear and the violence and pain around you, then dawns the Light more steadily and you have reached a place where you can choose instead of remaining asleep, alone in the dark.

When you choose the Word and place it in the center of what may seem to you a vault of darkness, you make the beginning that will set you free. This is a parable; understand it, for when you fall into neglect back cometh the twilight which grows darker until you are again in darkness.

No wonder it is a re-enacting of birth out of darkness into life, into resurrection.

This is a solemn instruction. You in this center alone can never stay in one place; you either sink down or are uplifted, for when you neglect the Word in days of freedom you will find your sky darkening. . . . Keep in the Word for your life's sake, for your love's sake.

This is a time for dedication, a time for baptism, for sanctification. No matter what happens remember not to allow the twilighting of your sky; keep illumined in the Word and let your battle cry be, "I am the Light of the world!"

. . . *The great Prince of Peace and spirits, as He comes forth, casts a cloud about Him; so He comes on upon us; so He encompasseth us. . . . Yet still we speak of Him as far above and beyond the starry sky, and of His coming as at a great distance. But, behold! He is already in the midst of us; He breaks forth on our right hand, and on our left, like a flame, round about us, and we perceive Him not.*

Peter Sterry [Cromwell's Chaplain], d. 1671

I N THESE DAYS OF VIOLENCE IT IS IMPORTANT TO BEAR A standard upon the side of righteousness in your daily lives and to remember that fear is the tempter, that it is faith in your antagonist as I have told you before. It is the destroyer and always brings sorrow.

One can have nothing but compassion for those who dwell in fear but we would lead them away into the only place of trust and protection. As he said, "This kind goeth out only by fasting and prayer." Therefore pray, keep your body a holy temple for only then can the flaming powers pour through.

Use your imagination to realize that the hidden strengths within you are awakened sometimes through great experiences, shocks, changes. Man is aroused to manhood or broken very often by lack of courage, spiritual courage which could have been his for the asking. There are those all over the world today who are giving testimony of having received what they asked for simply, with childlike faith. It is simplicity that is hard for us. But you have found a way through the darkness as they, in terrible need, have done; you too, in your everyday lives, can take your lamp and walk quietly step by step down a path into lighted confidence. Keep it lighted, never let it go out. Those others who are hard pressed by grim circumstances do not have to be reminded to watch their light; it is their life, the Almighty, the Comforter.

. . . The human reality has a terrifying grip and faith seems very nebulous when danger's breath is hot on your face, but your safety is in letting go to faith and in knowing that faith is where your mind is. Give yourself up to it, let go, for underneath are the everlasting arms. It is true that you cannot speak of faith as if it were an abstract or medicinal sort of thing; no, it's the actual touching of Christ himself.

Goodness is not goodness unless it is a rapture.

Robert Norwood, 1874-1932

YOU KNOW YOUR INSTRUCTIONS, FOR WHATEVER WE TELL you is forever the same simple manual. It may be told to you in many ways, yet it all resolves down to the eternal role or principle, if you will have it so. Everyone has a divine spark and it is realized for the most part, forgotten often. All we bring to you is the prayer, the sympathetic suggestion that you keep it alight. Blow on it until it becomes a reality, for it will consume and burn away dross. Many have to go through suffering to be awakened, but that is the human way, not the divine way which is one of illumination when we seek and ask as if it were more important than anything else in life. Every experience changes us one way or another. When the spark is neglected it naturally grows duller and then untoward circumstances, personalities, difficulties, obstructions, steal us away into forgetfulness and we put the emphasis of our vitality, thought and enthusiasm upon outward events which seem so important at the moment. Where are the events of yesterday that engaged our time and minds out of all proportion to their importance? Your first task is to blow upon your divine spark and each one is alone with himself in this regard. It isn't enough that we come together and receive renewed strength, surcease and inspiration; the battle is alone with yourself in a material world.

You have the instructions, you have the chart, the course is laid. It is for you now at this great time to dedicate your inward life to the manifestation of that which is invisible, this secret personal industry. You will come away with refreshment, encouragement and help from your common communion, but the actual work is yours alone. A man turns to his beloveds for comfort, healing and renewed strength, the strong family ties. But he faces life and its struggle alone and if he is illumined from within and cleaves with all his might to his inward inspiration his reward is a sense of eternal brotherhood with the invisible and the companionship of him who never leaves nor forsakes. And for every victory and step forward into this regeneration of your human selves, so much are we and all the world inspired in ways you may not yet understand. No one can take a step ahead of you or lay down your lives for you, but for every noble impulse, for every action obedient to your voice within, you are given strength.

You seem to forget at times to use your greatest gift in ordinary human conflicts and problems and are forever leaving out the essential approach, which is very understandable in a life of worldliness. But your opportunity is great now for the worldly are bewildered and shaken. Bring this light within you into your eyes and hands and feet, into your comings and goings, into every small effort, for the more you use it the more wonderful will be your reward.

And so I tell you that you have the knowledge, and the chart and the implements for your journey upward, onward through this frightened world. Blow upon your spark within, keep still in multitudes, hold your mind there and keep it from racing and do not beat against life with frantic effort; the quiet effort is toward awareness, keeping cool and unruffled, in perfect faith, in celestial stillness in your daily lives.

> *By all means use sometimes to be alone,*
> *Salute thyself: see what thy soul doth wear.*
> *Dare to look in thy chest: for 'tis thy own:*
> *And tumble up and down what thou find'st there.*
> *Who cannot rest till he good fellows find,*
> *He breaks up house, turns out of doors his mind.*
>
> George Herbert, 1593-1632

WE HAVE SAID BEFORE THAT IN THESE TIMES YOU MUST BE sure not to establish too deep an interest in events so that you are a barometer to news. It is, of course, a part of the life you live, but do not be drenched in the shocks which come suddenly in these days of violence, for one must stay held in his hand without being lured or tempted away by despair. Stay in your high tower of quiet while in action.

This admonition can be misunderstood; all about you are those who will say, "Surely this is a form of egotism, of exaggerated self-importance, an escape. You are trying to pull down the blinds and shut out realities which we all ought to face; it is smug and does not have sympathy for your fellow man. You shut a door upon what you ought to know."

Nothing is further from the truth. This way of life is not egotistical, because it is only successful when we put ourselves aside completely by saying, "Of myself I can do nothing." There is no exaggeration of the self because that spells instant failure of accomplishment. It is not an escape because it is the way of service, the constant acknowledgment of responsibility to your fellow man through realization of your obligation to him. You do not pull down the blinds when you turn your face to God, that you may abide in his presence and bring his peace nearer than the despair of the world. You are not making yourselves smug and self-righteous when you "make your being as wide as eternity" that you may be a channel for him to pour through his healing love to the world; and no one faces reality with more profound awareness than the person who looks upon it with the eyes of compassion that see through the wrong to the invincible Right brooding near, waiting to be used, to pour out itself in abundant joy.

You have been taught to "seek *first* the kingdom" and it is sometimes hard, because of our inherited belief that duty must be a trial, to believe that joy comes first; goodness, truth and beauty come first. Selflessness is a more-of-God-ness. "I will sing unto the Lord as long as I live!" . . . and it is that singing note that we hear from within that fortress across the seas today. Facing terror, they sing; and it is through such singing God works.

Have no fear; turn within to that eternal stillness where abides spiritual strength. It is then your cup runneth over and spills itself throughout the universe, it is a bounty poured out to mankind. Nothing is too big nor too little, for you do not yet know enough of values nor your latent power. But you *do* know from human experience the power of the despair spirit, the discouraged spirit, the ironic spirit. Therefore of how much greater power is your mustard seed of faith. Refuse all else, be undismayed, at peace in the center of the immortality within yourself, for this is helping to bring order out of chaos. Don't think too much how it is to be done, and do not be afraid to be like children under the wings of the Almighty.

Let no darkening thought put out one lamp, and this year of all years, worship the Babe in the manger with thanksgiving and joy for he is the Light of the world. The holy mystery is that his spirit dwells within us, and his word is, "*Let* your light shine!"

                                        Christmas, 1943

Sometimes the body sits on a stump and has to be told by the happy Spirit, March on, brave one!

                                        Anonymous

Man impelled by his natural foresight inclines toward his own perfection.

                                        Dante Alighieri, 1265-1321

Fulfil thyself in perfection through Me.

Anonymous

Jones Very said he felt it an honor to wash his face, being, as it was, the temple of the Spirit.

Emerson's *Journal*

౨

D O YOU NOT BEGIN TO SEE WITH THE INWARD EYE, REALIZING at last the reality of the spiritual intent? The thought beneath the threshold is uncovered a little and you are able to perceive with a clearer vision the meaninglessness of your human desires—inertias, angers, prides and all the heavier attributes of character. As you stand here truth will shine in dark places and you will find that a new faculty will appear, as it were, within you, and you will hear because of the refinement of your nature through this fasting, the clear and delicate whisper which once heard and obeyed will give you the kingdom. Through the overcoming of appetites you are a new awakened entity (it is indeed a rebirth) able at last to hear the voice which has spoken to you so often but was faint because of the obstruction of the impulses and desires of the outer you. The secret is that by becoming one with the invisible through spiritual knowledge, through continence in all things, you free yourselves from heavy burdens which are soul-destroying, and you can go through fire without being burned. Be holy, be holy, be exquisite instruments—in all humility be kings!

You have heard and obeyed. Many get comfort in the hearing and do not obey. There is a strange place in the thick realm between the hearing of the word and the assimilation of it—the acting upon it. You go into cul-de-sacs, sleeps of forgetfulness; often we want to shake you out of your sleep into realization. Many appetites act like opium and blur the crystal-clear vision that is needful. Obey the words of the Spirit; watch the outer you, keep him from interfering, and that is a task you cannot go to sleep in.

It is an extraordinary goal you would achieve and requires vigilance. The causes of buffetings are not revealed to man except in glimpses as he pushes on in high faith, in action; for you have to *live your way out.* Remember that your past efforts are with you to help you in your daily crisis,[1] and often when the way about you is dark look down and you will find your feet are on shining ground, the golden road is solid under your feet. The artist simile is very apt, ponder on it if you wish to be spiritual beings of a high order; to become so in a very real and tragic world—tragic in the sense that it is a world human, selfish and ignorant—the artist faces all those things, he knows his goal and is not satisfied with second-rate efforts, for there is nothing second class in true art. There is a fine strength in holding yourselves to the work in hand, for nothing worth while achieved in the realm of spirit or of art has been done softly in the thickness of the outer coatings.

We are trying to tell you that the escape from pain and violence is to release the inner you from the prison of the outer you, for when you let this divine spirit free so that it is in every action of your living day you will be healed, comforted, assured with a sense of safety in the lofty realm of truth and beauty, order and proportion—free in a high impersonal selfless life. Free, as Paul said, from the law of sin and death; and by escaping the law is meant the tendencies of your character when it sinks into its human self. You always loved the truth, and it is strong stuff. But we are trying to say that the beautiful, childlike thing to do is exquisitely joyful—hold yourself in a listening attitude and be artists in Christ.

[1] A literal translation from the Greek of Matt. 12:36 is, "That every idle word that men shall speak they shall give account thereof on the (their) day of crisis."

> *Miracles are not contrary to nature but only contrary*
> *to what we know about nature.*
>
> St. Augustine, A.D. 353

✑

IN THIS TIME OF GREAT STORMS OF FEELING, MOVEMENTS OF
psychic forces, hatreds, passions, merciless terror, the agony
of self-preservation and misunderstanding . . . here you stand.
It is the moment for you to realize that when you open to receive the spirit of the mind of Christ you let into this maelstrom of feeling, a north wind to cool the heat and clear the
skies and to know that you can be a means of bringing sanity
and lifting hope. Oh see the vision! This is helping to overcome the world.

In the galaxy of thoughts that makes your mind you have
the imagination of the seeing eye, the eye that perceives the
invisible; keep a childlike hopeful knowledge of the unseen
goodness and a surety that the divine principle can be
reached; remember that though you may be very small outwardly you can be as the universe, your mind is limitless. Realize your cosmic powers and take time to be a channel for the
infinite Spirit to pour through in this great war against darkness, inertia and savagery. As you walk your way and go about
your little daily lives, *be measureless,* be timeless, be eternal.
Thus will you begin at this time, at this place to fulfill the
prophecy, "Thy kingdom come, Thy will be done, on earth
as it is in heaven."

. . . My children, cultivate the habit of remembering that
in the spiritual world there is no time; in doing this the relative values will be better understood. It is a great help to take
the long view, thus throwing faith far ahead of you upon
your path, making the road safe. The next step is practical
also—take no thought of anxiety; sufficient unto the day is

both the goodness and the evil thereof. And this means that each day is in miniature your whole life. Take it as a complete period to be lifted high and you will have the sense of something already achieved, something built around you for your protection. See how you can shape the whole day—and then the summation of the long view is shaped also. The psychologist may tell you this is habit forming; he is wrong. It is on an entirely different plane. If you take each day and lift it to the highest you can reach, knowing that each day's problems will be solved spiritually, you will be given almost direct action . . . changing water into wine!

The power given you when you wake in the morning with this thought will be tremendous in this time of crisis. When you first wake, you are born, and you live a life as the day proceeds until you sleep again. The overtone, your high thought and intent is your direction for the twenty-four hours. Say, "I am here, Lord, and I will follow thee and thy guidance and listen with an inward ear." And again say to yourself, "I shall try and understand that I am reborn this day. Though I have been here I have never been here before. I will forget yesterday and I shall not dwell upon tomorrow. I will live my span in this miniature sample of a lifetime." In doing this you will have revealed to you yourself. And what is revealed is—how much do you literally believe and obey the inner voice?

Try to make manifest the living Presence once in the twelve hours. Resolve every time you are reborn to make God a reality at least once. And the way is not by hurling yourself at the idea from a sense of duty, but by dissolving into the limitless space within you where there are no restrictions, where there is no poverty, no pain, but where there is peace, the infinite love and salvation . . . *a safe return,* as that word truly means.

... God doth not ride me as a horse, and guide me
I know not whither myself; but converseth with me
as a Friend; and speaks to me in such a dialect as I
understand fully, and can make others understand.

Henry More, 1614-1687

Y OU OFTEN WONDER WHY IT HAS TAKEN SO LONG FOR
certain events to be realized in your lives; that is your question. This is the answer: how long has it taken you to obey
the simple requests given you? Has much been asked? Has
anything been demanded beyond your strength and intelligence? Let us be spiritually honest; you ask, you pray for results; do you spiritually work for them? Honestly, have you?

I do not like the word "work"—it is too hard a word. But
above all, above all, this is not a happy anodyne, an escape
from the realities of life through which you can be pleasantly
rested and released from momentary strains; this is not an
opiate. You have never been failed when you have wholeheartedly opened to receive the Spirit that abides within you;
opened to receive it into your mind, into your heart by transmuting all untoward emotions through it. We see this lack of
active co-operation so often when great wisdom has been
manifested to those who asked for it, and even while receiving it, it slipped away and was forgotten and the advice not
taken. The thing enjoyed was the moment of spiritual awareness and the wonderment that the glory for an instant was
felt.

How often it is said, "How true and beautiful are these
communions!" and then they are not acted upon very much,
if at all. This is not a chiding; it is an answer to your question,
"Why, oh why am I in this or that situation?" You are a

human organism and spiritual intelligence is difficult to assimilate and realize. You see the failures more clearly in your acquaintances when they fail to act upon their inner wisdom.

All that is asked is an awareness of God's awareness of you, of the immense love of his spirit for you. There is no *must* nor effort in this, for once the heart is touched by an awareness of him it is comforted, reassured, content.

No effort brings this confident companionship; it is a gift given to him who takes time to rest in the desire for Him, and will free himself from delaying appetites, not always physical appetite. There are greeds that stand in your way; not just the outer greed, but the quality of the spirit of greed within: *there* is where the refinement must take place; melt away this murky darkness which so intimately surrounds the lighter spirit.

The spiritual significance of baptism, the ancient ritual of crowning a king, hold true; the linen shirt before the gold tunic and the crown. Realize your dedication and you will be free; you cannot hold great power without hurting yourselves if you are full of great shadows and fears. Be holy! Inward discipline is close to the quick of life eternal, and we tell you that the high purity of the light you seek must be made way for. Ah, I have it . . . clean the lamp chimney so the light can shine through! It is not difficult when done with joy and good sense. Ask of yourselves the subtle refinement; to hate a man, to self-justify, to overeat, to walk through the day in a subjective sleep, to roll an appetite upon the tongue. . . . Go to the root, what do you want most?

Do not be the ones to receive great inspirations and not act upon them; rededicate your lives and by love and not effort, clean your lamps.

Narrow is the mansion of my soul; enlarge Thou it, that Thou mayest enter in.

St. Augustine, A.D. 353

∽

IT MAY BE HELPFUL FOR YOU TO CONSIDER THE FACT THAT TO permit stupid thoughts to dwell and slip through the mind is as dangerous as to let sharp delicate tools slip through the fingers. Therefore the old practice of self-examination is recommended if it is made with clean, concentrated thinking that challenges one's words and deeds during the miniature life of a day, thus planning for the future. See and realize the strange unreasonable elements that seem to come from nowhere; shades of savagery born from self-pity, the constant oversweet voice that indulges the self, condoning excuses. There is much degeneration due to emotional storms, even though they are secret storms, that needs the strong tools of creative, intelligent thought to clear away. Yes, build yourselves a practical, efficient, spiritually-hard working instrument that will live your life for you more easily, in balance, so that you will walk sure-footedly through states of emotion. When you are stung by a hurt, an unreasonableness, a delay, watch your response; take it out and look at it. You are to think your way out. Now that you are more aware of divine assistance, cease from being fools, for the wise man is he who when he prays for wisdom and receives it, acts upon it. Many pray, receive and do not recognize it. Pray that you may realize the tools of thought—recognize them—when they are put shining into your hands. There are no excuses in this realm.

This is not preaching in the old scolding way; this is awakening in your consciousness the inspiration of knowing that you can overcome the world; you cannot overcome the world by formless prayer, although I would not confuse you by implying that you have to put prayer always into words. It is the deep intent, the idea, that carries power; the shape of a cup shapes the substance it contains. That is why the emotion behind a word does not always bring what we expect or desire. It is not enough to say "my kingdom is not of this world." That is a truth, a noble and divine theme, a statement of intent. What matters is how are you going to prove there is a kingdom within you in which you are a crowned king? Your life is not placed in a palace, but in a very restricted, irritated small area of reality where you meet the heat and cold of public opinion, delays and obstructions, jealousies, malice, lacks, boredom and strain. It is not enough to say "my kingdom is not of this world" and not arrange your thoughts accordingly. An awakening is taking place, a dawning, for the time is approaching when you will realize that you cannot advance spiritually unless you act upon the wisdom given you, instead of receiving, of hearing the voice and then doing nothing about it.

Out of the race has come such realizations because every human who has made this journey has come to this place, this time of understanding, when he sees that by acting upon the revelation that has come to him is the only way he can win to victory.

Here is a prayer for thy comfort: "I stand in the light of the Spirit knowing that this tired flesh is not the reality of myself. In this light I stand, aware of immortality now. I will dedicate my waking hours to the realization of this Presence and the knowledge that I am never alone. Thou art with me always and thou art my refreshment."

There is only one Wisdom; it is to understand the thought by which all things are steered through all things.

                                        Heraclitus, 500 B.C.

My will in thee is faith, not fear; let My will within thee be done.

My will in thee is Wisdom, not foolishness; let My will within thee be done.

My will in thee is Health not disease; let My will within thee be done.

My will within thee is thy awareness of My love for thee; let My will within thee be done.

Joy,—you understand so little of the joy of Life! You perform so many of your daily avocations as burdensome tasks instead of labours of love. Be like little children filled with secret wonder and joy and the spirit of high adventure.

M. A. W.

❧

IN THE YOUTHFUL MOMENTS OF TRIUMPH WHEN YOU KNEW the race was to be won you found one kind of satisfaction; in the hilarious confidence which came through successful attainment you found another; the serenity which came from a sense of security was still another. Now, when many things are seemingly turned against you, you are faced with the age-old antagonist which is called adversity. It has been met before.

In facing realities out there with your physical and outer consciousness you are challenged with old humors, fears, dismays and your world is frozen into immobility. In this adventure, where you have barely crossed the threshold, much preparation which may have seemed slow and useless has taken place. Listen then, listen and receive. Face your enemy with your outer selves; do not think, listen; listen and repeat these words; put them in your mouth and blow them like a clarion, high and sweet and clear to the four corners; "My kingdom is not of this world. I will abide in my kingdom and as the

day followeth the night my kingdom shall be made manifest
and my outward life shall straighten and fall into a divine
mold."

You do not see the immediate manifestation because you
are still children, and as a child's destiny is locked in its
breast, so you, by this spiritual communion are unlocking
prisons that you are unaware of in material life; blind as you
are to the immediate development you should see clearly the
happy radiance of your freedom from the laws of your outer
worldliness. Through obedience you can find dominion, so
do not waste your time in outward fret; you have not been
prepared for that form of activity. Through spiritual loyalty
and heavenly enthusiasm you can be prepared for the kingdom of happiness upon this tortured and suffering earth. Indeed, indeed he will "give you beauty for ashes."

This is to remind you that he who is God's anointed shall
nevermore quail; give me your hands and repeat these words:
"Blessed Saviour here I stand and here I reaffirm my vow with
all the strength of my body, my soul, my mind; I vow that I
will put thee first, that I will endeavor to bring my thought,
my brain, my heart, my very flesh and blood to the instant
realization of thy actual holy presence within me. I dedicate
myself to the realization of you, my Redeemer, my Comforter,
in every action of the day or night. I vow that I will challenge
every experience that cometh to meet me; my whole life I
dedicate to the realization of thy word. I vow to keep my body
pure, my mind sweet and ready for thy intent, knowing that I
rest in thy immortal love."

∽

IT WAS PROMISED THAT IN OBEDIENCE TO THE WORDS GIVEN, YOU
would be protected and held together, held from your own
scatterings. You know well enough that you make your human
difficulties yourselves through your unawarenesses. Now re-

member this, you will each be safe and protected within the fortress of your own making; therefore we ask you to draw within and stay there. This drawing within and staying involuntarily controlled is a task for those who would be masters of their material and spiritual lives, self-contained in God. You are tired, for you have let your armor slip from you, and you have a sense of futility; that is understandable, for the spiritual way, which is new to the race (compared to the ways of human experience) is difficult for the mind to remember. Here we are, telling the same story as in the beginning! Let us examine ourselves; what is the holy grail we seek? We seek absolute dominion over life; that is the long adventure, the direction and the purpose. We seek the wisdom, the knowledge and the intelligence to face and eliminate from our characters those weaknesses and inertias, fears and lukewarmnesses which bring about that state in affairs wherein we have no dominion, but are enslaved by those who have more intelligence and strength, even though they are still on a lower plane.

Facing the realities, therefore, you will agree that we must play this game of the will-to-win as one plays a game of tennis; with the concentrated one-pointedness of the will to succeed, to surmount all difficulties, to keep emotions calm, serene; to keep from anger which immediately gives the antagonist the advantage. In this game it is necessary to keep joyous in understanding love, to keep faithful because that is where your heart is, inspired, transcended, that you may know yourself as a son of God. When you affirm this joyous and indomitable resolution and keep yourself involuntarily within yourself, calm, sure, undismayed, unafraid—then you will not scatter and be at the mercy of the violences and the jealousies, the humiliations and dullness of stupid events.

Those who are faithful and aware of the companionship of the Spirit, those who know they do not walk alone through the violence of these times, know also that the steadfastness given them by the Spirit when they are channels for it, helps mightily to strengthen the unity of the whole, even though fear and peril stalk the earth.

Rise up and shout within yourselves for this state of dominion and perform what should be normal results instead of passive fumbling at an idea. What we call normal results by making this principle work you call a miracle. The time has come for you to march against this tide of darkness and carry your lighted lamps quietly, steadily. Heal yourselves, your bodies, your characters; get out of this slough of indefiniteness and bewilderment; come in where you belong and give this tragic world the infinite qualities of the Spirit when you let it have its way with you as channels for joy, beauty and truth. You are spiritual beings, you are great and noble people *when* you are your divine selves. Now stand up in the center of your unregenerated selves and be born again. Be miracle workers, pierce the clouds, pierce high heaven and Light will come pouring through; for he is thy friend, he is thy comforter, he is thy teacher, thy solace, thy strength, thy impersonal, eternal Reality.

Now is the appointed time; rise and be illumined, rise and be awake, knowing that your hands are uplifted. His wisdom is in thy heart, his strength is in thy body, and in this state of grace, ask what ye will and it will be done unto you, pressed down and overflowing. You have sensed this is the truth, now make the truth a reality.

All the great works and wonders that God has ever wrought . . . or even God Himself with all His goodness, can never make me blessed, but only in so far as they exist and are done and loved, known, tasted, and felt within me.

Theologia Germanica, 1497

*They that observe lying vanities forsake their own
mercy.*

                                                    Jonah 2:8

✍

IT MAY HELP YOU TO REMEMBER ONCE IN AWHILE HOW DEEPLY
the human being is enmeshed in the flesh, and, what is not
often thought of, the flesh is very old. Although it is constantly renewed in an almost incredibly short time, a few
months, the cells bear the stamp of race memories and experiences of the ages past and that is why this tired flesh, the
body of the human race, which has met savagery, war, sorrow
and grief, is so friendly to despair.

Now you, in times of peace, were given a standard to carry
and you chose the lonely road; seemingly lonely. It is lonely
because of cynicism and disbelief, which is part of the race
memory you carry with you as a member of this physical body
of the human race, so old, so inert, that it gives off clouds of
doubt and fear. For this reason it is difficult for some to look
upon the pure innocence of a new idea without suspicion.

You have received this idea and entertained it at intervals,
and between the intervals the clouds that emanate from old
habits of thought obscure the light and you walk about in a
sleep of forgetfulness until you remember and you come again
to fitfully hold in awareness the illuminating Spirit. Yet I tell
you that this Light is more powerful than the past and the
heavy race record that is written upon it. Although fitfully
held it has protected and safeguarded your lives, for this communion that you hold is very powerful, though how this is
so is strange to your human conception. The simplest metaphor is that you are a lamp, for you can become illumined
and the invisible rays of light that shine through your even

fitful awareness, touch elements of which you have no knowledge. The world picture is baffling and dismaying; but as you dispel the miasmas and mists that arise from the ancient bogs of race experience, this inner light will free you from attributes that you have not realized. And this steadfast desire to know God and eternal life by faithful self-discipline is a greater offering to the hope of a new world than you can yet imagine. I tell you that by keeping steadily, rhythmically alive in faith, that beautiful eternal stillness where courage also dwells, you make an immeasurable contribution to mankind; quiet, unseen, unknown except to yourself. This will keep you from vain imaginings which find breeding grounds in the ancient swamps of past consciousness. Because you have this gift of the Spirit, your responsibility is great. You have this inward splendor; now use it!

Be vigilant in calmness; in love be there at your center. It is difficult, for one catches anxiety, irritation and fear, but if the race had done this it would not be at war. Be ahead of the race, not in its warlike preparations, but in the idea back of it, for you are the army of spiritual soldiers behind the actual ones, therefore your discipline in some ways must be sterner; not stern, perhaps, for love is the word; the edges of your intent must not be blurred. Remember that you are protected by your inner convictions.

"I, a son of God, stand in this human turmoil holding the long trust. I throw my trust, like light far ahead upon my path knowing that goodness and all that is merciful is with me and by this stand I do my share to make the world hoped for. In courage and in the love of God is the only safety."

> *I would fain be to the Eternal Goodness, what his own hand is to a man.*
>
> *Theologia Germanica,* 1497

W E HAVE FREQUENTLY TALKED TO YOU ABOUT THE disciplines of life, and I would like to make my meaning a little clearer. First of all do not be self-conscious about self-discipline for then it is easy to become self-righteous. The advice is, take action but be silent, for the real purpose is to awaken your faculties to a clean awareness of the reality of the Spirit. Let everything you do be toward that goal . . . *everything*. But for the sake of your personal lives do not do it too eagerly, do it silently, easily as breathing, and thoughtfully. Fast from too much talk (as well as food) in things spiritual; you will be told when to speak.

No one can tell you very much about the disciplining of the mind; it must come from a searching, honest examination of one's tendencies of thought and emotion. You know better than anyone can tell you of the accumulation of dreary mental luggage that you carry about with you; old prejudices, criticisms, foolish habits or response to ideas as well as surrounding influences, and mind-drifting; driftings toward nothing at all. But after I say this to you I realize that there is a danger in it, for if you become self-conscious about pleasant wanderings of the mind through the green pastures of your daily life, which bring a rich sense of appreciation, you may question it. I can illustrate what I mean by giving you a negative picture; if you receive bad news, if your mind is shaken by what you call righteous indignation or if you are suddenly afraid—you know instantly what to do, you turn to the divine Companion who walks with you, for help, wisdom and protection. We often need the drillmaster to keep us from dwelling too long in the subjective no-man's-land, but how you do this must come from your own experience within.

What is it you really want? You want to be brilliantly aware, gloriously alive with true health, sustained by omniscient wisdom and protected by steadfast faith. You want a healthy mind and spirit. Be assured that if you obey the promptings from within you will come into a new lease of vitality, power and happiness. Do not be discouraged by the stubbornness of the self, the ebbing tides of interest, and the sloughs of despond. Awake; so little is asked, so great is the reward!

Yes, here there is no confusion; here the surface of the water of life is not ruffled, here it is still and deep with eternal peace. The grandeur of the stillness that you find here will overcome all outward disturbances. Your task is not to throw fat into the fire. You are to be still, tenacious, faithful, that you may be an impersonal channel for the outpouring of wisdom and peace. As one said, "When you meditate open not only your listening mind but the other door of your mind as well so that eternal love streams out as fast as it comes in. Store nothing. Go into the calm and luminous silence to renew, but stay in the soil of your life for your strength. Do not waste time asking for peace; get more fearless peace into your souls, then you will be some good—and peace will follow."

∽

FOR WHAT CAN WE GIVE PRAISE, FOR WHAT CAN WE GIVE thanks, for what can we rejoice at this time? Let us not use these words lightly, nor fail to look in the face of suffering and dread as they walk the earth. The question is not, Why do they fill the world today? They have always been here; do not confuse quantity with quality, in suffering or in anything else. Jesus walked amidst violence and savagery and yet he said, "Ask that your joy may be full!" It is the same age-old question, not Why, but How are we to meet the invasion of our hearts and minds by the bitterness of the world? Down the ages comes the answer, over and over again, in many tongues, from all the steadfast ones: "For when the enemy shall come in like a flood the Spirit of the Lord shall lift up a standard against him," and the standard has to be lifted first in the heart, through our awareness of our oneness with the indwelling Christ, reborn daily within us in our resolution, in our courageous action, in the constant renewing of our minds and in a fiery faith. To everyone comes the angel with "the glad tidings that that Holy Thing which shall be born of thee shall be called the Son of God," and each is born not alone, but with the symbols of fortitude and loyalty, of faith and humility of love and protection standing near, as they stood near him in a stable, if our eyes can read the signs.

Yes, and you who have ears unstopped can listen and hear if you will. It is difficult for us to awaken you to your full opportunity, we cannot shake you into realization of the way you should go for your own protection, for your beloveds, for the world, but we have tried to give you a sort of manual to train yourselves to keep young, fluent, and full of faith; for human events so charged with emotion and terror are very difficult to manage if one has no manual nor the divine advantage. The little people drift down into a sleep, turn their faces from realities, so that when they are confronted with cruelty and savagery they lose their balance and add to the general weight of despair; they have not made their faith an actuality. Do not think this is a selfish protection for your own bodies and souls, we tell you that it is a dedication to the way that will bring healing and peace. When you walk in immortality there is neither big nor little, and when you "deny yourself" by making clear the way for the Spirit, you are giving Light to the world—giving It when of yourself you do nothing. What is asked of you is to keep this Light burning bright in quietness and to carry your illumination with you always. *Your lamp must not go out*, and it will not if you obey your childlike instinct. This is no time to beat one's hands against doors of brass, to rage at injustice, human evil and materialism; lift your hearts high above the storms of hatred and fear. A great role can be yours if you will be simple, and in all tenderness and love and assurance we ask you again to stand in the Light and not waver. You cannot understand events and their causes but you do know that keeping your emotional centers where they belong is your safety and by so doing you help profoundly in the regeneration that will come to pass. We ask that you prepare yourselves to be beacons.

We have heard you say you are tired of waiting. For your life's sake plunge into the immortal living Presence *now* and you will not "wait." One has said, "If thou dost every hour throw thyself by faith beyond all creatures, beyond all reasoning into the abyssal mercy of God, then thou shalt receive his power." Do you not see, do you not yet comprehend that Love within is the beginning of all things, and that you are forever beginning? Always renewing, always being reborn.

That is the eternal and holy gift, and in this time release thyself to the fullness of joy in the star that shines, in the Child that is born.

Christmas

᪘

LET US DURING THIS TIME RISE UP OUT OF THE VALLEY, OUT OF the plains, above the forest line, above the mountains into the clear air, into the realm where thought itself melts into instinct and is stilled. Open to receive and rest. . . .

After this refreshment I would recall to your remembrance the meaning of the spiritual law; how you obey it is your affair, we can only make suggestions and tell you not to be too much cast down when you do not receive, during these days of anxiety, all that you seek for in inspiration. When man seeks to perfect himself he always makes false starts and goes through intervals of disappointment, thoughtlessness and sleepwalking periods. Artists know this. How you need to work toward your goal is for you to discover and to decide, but we can tell you that nothing can release you so much as your awareness and sense of oneness with the presence of God. There is strength given you when you work out your own salvation; be self-reliant and stand alone and then the sharing will be added unto you as good measure. Today clothe yourselves in your invisible shining armor so that no evil shall come nigh your thought, and if you are tired, fast from news and idle talk. A sane austerity and self-discipline, if not carried too far, are good, for this eternal fight between the human and the divine nature is an eternal struggle. When you disobey your own divine desires you find yourselves uncomfortable, soiled and in need of a spiritual cleansing, so again we remind you to rise above the desert, the forest line, breathe the mountain air.

"O Holy Spirit, hold me in thy gentleness within, keep me from strain; keep me in thy radiant Presence, keep me awake and from the sleep of forgetfulness, keep me in remembrance of my immortality, of thy power within. I know that I am in thy love; keep me illumined and untarnished. Teach me to play my part. Amen."

⁓

IF YOU WILL OBSERVE WHAT HAS BEEN GIVEN YOU DURING THE past few years of your discipleship you will find that it is a quality of feeling to inspire you and give you faith and courage; a realization of the nearness of the Spirit of the Father. What is not revealed to you is the Why; why you were born at this time; why you met and chose this person or that one; why there is light and dark, why there is joy and pain. In a moment of dread and anxiety you turn to God in silence, as you have been inspired to do from the beginning, and even that is beyond you, also. Why you sense a quality of rest and comfort and assurance welling up within you in spite of the seemingly hopeless future of the human race is because hope is indeed eternal; it is a knowledge, a wisdom, it partakes of the nature of all eternal qualities. Your sense of comfort that comes to you by stilling thought does not come by your effort to still thought; you, rather, induce an active force instantly, and the less you think of how it works, the better it works, the stronger is the reassurance. You have nothing to fear, then, when you sit with a pure desire and a good heart in quietness and stillness. There are no words to tell of it because it is beyond the human experience of man and it is more powerful for good than all the contrivances of man for the destruction of man. There is nothing you can *think about* that is useful at this moment; be silent and you will be aware of the signs and wonders. You receive a luminous spirit and an anxious thought disappears; you have a still sense of comfort, of renewal, that is all there is. There is no sermon to be heard, no book to be read; it is all contained in "Be still and know that I am God." There is nothing else.

During these times, do not be drawn down suddenly into the pit of fear. Dismiss the alarm with all your might and main and keep to your illumined word. Let not dismay put out your lamp and loosen the scaffold of your resolution to abide forevermore in the Word that will set you free.

∽

YOU SAY THE DIFFICULT PROBLEM FOR YOU IS TO HOLD YOUR realization and not, after a communion, have it vanish. You want to keep your awareness, hold your soul. As you go on you will find this easier, like all habits, or pleasures, even. You will find the communions, the times of quiet meditation, an instructing experience. When you ask for wisdom for your daily living and truth for inspiration they will be revealed to you if you are steadfast. Truth is stern in its revelation and serene in realization and only in obedience will you be com-

forted. The sternness lies in your being awakened to your disordered and undisciplined states. Once again we return to the
simplicities and recall to your memory that in turbulent times
when the mind is image-making, you whip and drum up the
issues to such an extent that the excitement gets out of control and the mind and emotions race hysterically. Again we
tell you to sink down three fathoms below the storm, where
the stillness is; here where all things are accomplished, the
quiet where all things are done. When you come to the surface you will bring some of this calm, this undisturbed peace
with you; and the more you do this under stress, the more
involuntary it will become so that eventually your mind will
first seek the divine instead of human wisdom, which is largely
relative. Turn to the source for all needs and you will discover that your realization will last longer and longer between your journeys to the well of living water.

"O Christ dwelling within me, give me knowledge, knowledge of thyself in relation to my living, day by day. Give me
thy Spirit of eternal life to live now, on the earth, in the
elements, in the world. Feed my mind with thy living bread;
quench my thirst for thee with living water from the well of
life."

One of you has said, "It is hard for me to be still with
honest intent; my mind breaks into a thousand butterflies
when I reach forward to grasp the pearl of great price, and
when I reach out my hand to God my hand disappears and
I am over the hill and far away!" Indeed that is true of all
beginners. The only harm in it is believing it cannot be overcome—in accepting the idea that your mind cannot be won
if your heart desires it. But do not push, nor make an effort.
"Leave all quietly to God, my soul," for it is the gift of beauty
and comes only with joy. Realize that the emotional self is
not now the complete master; melt into the invisible serenity of
God in you and the healing rays will go forth doing the works.

*Let not him who seeks cease until he finds, and when
he finds he shall be astonished. Astonished he shall
reach the Kingdom, and having reached the Kingdom
he shall rest.*

Traditional Sayings of Jesus

∽

THERE IS A TEMPTATION FOR THE SO-CALLED REASONABLE
mind to be suspicious of this escape to a dream place. But
where else can you escape? Where else are things born? In the
states that confront the world at this time the confusion is
augmented if you have within you a spirit of anger and resentment and if you hold grimly to the accomplishment hoped
for. When you come within, come wholly; make your resolution before you come, and then leave, when you come, all else
behind. Come into this transcendent place of creative peace
and light . . . then it will be done. The Spirit you seek helps
you to be faithful and will hold you to your gains, and the old
challenges, which you face personally and nationally, can only
be met in this way by those who seek the truth. The freedom
that comes from the renunciation of materialism, to be loosened
from fear of lack when there is lack, are experiences which have
come to all those who have sought dominion; it is the way to
protection. The spiritual place that you reach in your communions is the gateway to that freedom; pass through naked
and you will not be hurt, you will be taken care of.

You have undertaken a homeric task, for the world and all
in it are suffering from soul sickness; the air you breathe is
full of it, of anxiety and pain, of hysteria and savagery; but
those who can find safe haven in the spiritual awareness of
their own godhood, awareness of the Spirit within them, not
only stand near to the love of God but lift the race with them.
Whenever you draw near to the secret place you do not go

entirely alone; you take mankind with you. It is one way of serving your neighbor. It is never a selfish thing, for by the healing and renewing of your own spirit you send out light to all consciousness. This is as scientific as the fact that in the physical world you cannot lift your hand without vibrations caused by your gesture being felt throughout it. How infinitely more is felt the victories of the inner you, into what far reaches of darkness in another may your light shine without a spoken word!

What are the servants of the Lord but His Minstrels.
St. Francis of Assisi, 1182-1226

ꮥ

LET US CONSIDER THE PAST YEARS WHEN IN THE BEGINNING WE met through these communions; like children you half believed it, it remained to you as definite as a story in symbol, instantly forgotten. You were brought back again and led away by events, the little events of daily life; great events bring you back quickly, but inertias smother you. Within the mind the spiritual entity was nebulous, out of focus, but it has gradually become more defined and this communion easier, yet it is still difficult for you to live your daily lives in awareness always of the infinite beauty that never leaves you, no matter if the mind is turned away from it. The magnet of the life about you, what you call actuality, is so absorbing the contact is broken, though for shorter periods, and the divine power is now so established that it draws you back, but it would be well for you to study yourselves objectively in this matter. This awareness should not be a divided thing, feeling him one time and then having long intervals of forgetfulness. It is rather that you feel him within you, beside you and about you actually while in different environments. Keep the contact if you can as an undertone or overtone; carry your stillness with you. Instead of walking with God you so often walk with feverish thought which tires you and lowers your vitality and resistance. Where are the thoughts of yesterday, last month, last year? Where are the busy exciting interests of the past decade gone?

You know that the communions in stillness have not gone, they have remained, each adding more and more power and understanding to the realization of the living Presence; this you bear witness to, that each withdrawal from the world of appearances to the world of eternal love has been a building of a structure, a living invisible temple not made with hands, and each withdrawal was a stone chiseled and squared that you placed in position until the edifice is high and strong and good. Yes, indeed silence, profound silence, deeper than thought, deeper than your five senses, deeper than any experience you have known will grow more and more powerful and the Word will be made flesh to heal and straighten your lives and bring you abundance of peace in these days of war. Do not underestimate how important this is, for by living with this divine source of peace you help to restore it to the world. Abide in the very core, the secret place of the most High. No orders are given you, for this must be done through love which will give you inward fortitude. Be dismayed by nothing, keep this inward contact secure in your outward living for this is being in the ark of salvation, and this is the way to keep yourselves channels for the Spirit to pour through to those who walk in darkness. Hold your light high by being faithful and abiding in his words.

ᔆ

TODAY WE SPEAK OF THE REALIZATION OF THE BLACK AND white of daily living; now one thing and now another. See these states; they seem to come out of a bag and surround us. They are very real while they last, these times of fermentation and doubt. It seems to you that there can be no light or hope and the days are gray and dark. *Much of this is steam rising from you and you make your own fog.* When understood it is a sign of growth; but you will feel better, feel cleansed when you have the understanding to ponder on the strangeness of these states, as being unreal and not of truth. The healing of the spirit comes in these times of realization. Don't you begin to see that these moments are self-made and lie in your own responses? Your release lies in taking these moments, both the star moments and the nettles and in holding them in each hand while you consider them. By this act of the free will you become a master, for at last you take your appointed place in your own unfoldment.

This dwelling upon your own states is not a dangerous knitting of the brows in introspection, for there is no self-love in the process, neither is there pride nor self-pity. To know yourself you must become impersonal and selfless; then with that calm, impersonal knowledge which is given to you in cooling draughts, you will free and cleanse yourself of the states and the events which made them so very real and ungovernable. In this way you make yourself free; a little at a time perhaps, but you have discovered the principle and the rest follows.

Now do you not perceive that Christ in you cannot be apart like a phantom? No, no! He demands the outer you as well as your inner self to make the perfect whole.

You are here, now, at this place, at this time, in this room, in your world, in the scheme of this moment, and you have never been at this moment before. Well, then, take this moment and instead of letting it wing through the mind as nothing, receive it as a divine gift and place it in the chalice, holding it up as high as you can reach. That is how you help all other persons at their stations—now at this moment. See nations this way; open and enlarge the realization of each moment; enlarge the *now.* This is how inspiration will pour into your life for, oh, it is so important not to drop the moments on the floor! Hold them up into the light when all the currents and tides are against you; every time you raise a low impulse to the highest, those nearest you are lifted and changed. In this way are destructive emotions transmuted, like water into steam, a driving force for good. Nature demands lawlessly and hungrily and if indulged will consume and destroy you by her spendthrift lack of restraint.

Do you not see that by doing this you literally bring order out of chaos and create a new world? Nature is made to obey the great law that will uplift the human race.

By allowing the fear of being ineffectual to enter into the state of prayer and by wishing to accomplish something myself, I spoilt it all.

St. Jeanne de Chantel, 1572-1641

の

THE TIMES ARE VERY, VERY BIG AND POTENT. THE ONLY hope is to be bigger than the times and more potent. What needs to be realized is your own importance in the scheme. You have been told to stand to your full stature. This may sound silly to you, but if everyone did this, everything would be kept in its proper place, and beauty and order and rightness would fall out of the sky like magic. That is why reformers fail, they do not work from the inside out. If they would but look up into the sky above they could bring down the kingdom of heaven to this weary and bewildered earth!

Of course it is necessary to discipline the appetite for rage, emotional regrets, and all the things that rough and tumble life presents to you, but really there are only two things, the darkness of despair and greed, and the light of eternal joy— either black or white. By merely turning your face away from darkness to light you are in light and darkness does not exist for you. Mathematics! Impersonal and as clean as that. That is why it seems so stern to the sentimentalists who think God should do every little thing for them. No, each one has to go through the process of finding out that the fight of materialism, and all the cynical forces, is one where he or she fights alone, and the fight is choosing the idea, or awakening to the idea; and new ideas are always painful to the unspiritual.

Those who plan too well, like certain generals, never achieve in the hour of crisis. Those who plan too well are those who become in love with their own system.

Those who are creative, open, released, free, growing and alive will, in times of crisis, receive the great flashes of inspiration which save nations. All is in the approach. If you approach the spiritual growth by planning, you will delay your progress. But if you approach it in the true way you will find no obstruction. By falling in love with the spiritual state you will solve the riddle of how to be always aware of the Presence. That is the problem of you who are where you are now. It is as if, when unaware of that which you truly desire most, you stepped into black pockets and life is blank—out of order. Now Love is order; it is beauty, it is living mathematics. It is a vital organizer.

Another way to look upon this problem of your spiritual evolution is to regard your outer you as one you would educate. What are you trying to bring forth in this outer self?— a living consciousness of oneness with God. Look at this outer you as if he were a youth stepping forth into life delayed by temptations along the way, wasting noble gifts on nonessentials; lotus eating.

He finds himself in certain states of psychic sleep, of emotional cul-de-sacs which numb the imagination, often imprisoning it. What does your God want for this outer you? He wants you to hold him and lift him to his full height, shaking off inertia, indolence, drifting; for so much of the hurt and pain comes through omission—blank states. It is like the vacuum formed in the sky which brings about the tornado. Beware of vacuums! Fill them with light and the still, eternal, joyful spirit of a tender and loving God.

The stoics and religious fanatics went the outside way by fasting, by penance and by monastic routine. Many found peace of a kind, but the pearl of great price was not often theirs; the pearl of great price can be yours but for the loving.

Beware of the emotions that are hosts to violence.

M.A.W.

∽

TODAY WE WILL BE "PRACTICAL." IT IS TRUE THAT IF YOU have as much faith as a grain of mustard seed you will bring balance and order into your daily life. When you start a new enterprise you pray and you go on your way carrying your light. What happens? You meet other souls in different stages of their development, with different grades of intelligence and because of their strength, their ambitions and self-interests, you are bound to be in conflict. See this with the eye of reality, but never with criticism nor personal condemnation; for their lacks, their weaknesses of character are not your business and must not be regarded with self-justification or excuse. They, too, are on their way. Your problem is not to be immediately moved by the forces they let loose so that your light is blown out in the strain of adjustment and pressure. That is why faith is so hard to hold in the midst of lack of faith; but you must realize that your character, the galaxy of attributes which you call yourself, is either weakened or made stronger by the dismay among personalities when one is tempted to shrink into the darkness of fear.

Now, fear being the antithesis of faith, it can be used as one would use a force. When you go out in the morning to meet the old antagonist in the problems and personalities of the day, face it as a challenge, or, rather, as an angel to wrestle with, your weapon being your faith. The angel is the guardian to the gate of all faith, as it were. Perhaps he will speak through the mouths of many persons and you hear, "You cannot." "It is no use." "It will fail." "Why go on?" He is the examiner who tests your moral courage, your weapon of faith. Because you have let your mind be emotionally caught up so that it races, he will get under your guard and catch you unawares. Every man meets this in any endeavor. Perhaps I ought to make it clear that I do not mean an angel has been sent, nor that evil is goodness; but, like Jacob, you can make an angel of your antagonist who will bless you.

Consider a game of chess or tennis: in both you meet an antagonist and your will to win must dominate you, must control your skill so that if your guard is broken you will keep cool and vigilant. This overtone of feeling will co-ordinate your body involuntarily; and your sense of mastery, because of your will to win being paramount, will give inspiration and success. But if, because of a streak of bad playing, you are angered or excited, you will be thrown off your guard.

Let faith be the overtone of your day; faith and the rightness of your cause. Fill yourself with the light and illumination of the Spirit within you and go out into the material world where you will instantly meet the counter-plays of humans like yourself, seeking to win; some, perhaps, by hook or crook. Because of your mustard seed of faith, when rightly understood, you will by practice not lose your temper, not be dismayed, not let fear weaken your moral fiber and you will be inspired and made strong and your adversary will stand aside and open the gate because you have played honorably with yourself and with him, through your faith in your indwelling Wisdom and Power. It will be a victory far greater than the material consequences of your striving. Do not any

longer be sleepwalkers! This vigilance means complete awareness, an awareness of being illumined or in the dark.

Be dismayed by nothing. Watch the plays of your antagonist
with humor and good sportsmanship, and hold to your will
to faith; then is the time when all that is glorious can work
best for you. Study your moral fiber, ponder on this; faith is
infinite, infinite is his love.

> *I am sure there is a common Spirit that plays within
> us, yet makes no part of us; and that is the Spirit of
> God; . . . this is that gentle heat that broodeth on
> the waters and in six days hatched the world; this is
> that irradiation that dispels the mists of hell, the
> clouds of horror, fear, sorrow, despair; and preserves
> the region of the mind in serenity. Whatsoever feels
> not the warm gale and gentle ventilation of the
> Spirit (though I feel his pulse) I dare not say he lives;
> for truly without this, to me there is no heat under
> the Tropick; nor any light, though I dwell in the
> body of the sun.*
>
>   Sir Thomas Browne, 1605-1682

THERE IS AN OUTER RING OF YOURSELF SURROUNDED BY
turbulence, chaos and anxiety; great moments swirling
about, cosmic in potentiality. Within this ring is another
circle outside of which are your responses to all these alarms
and insistent shocks, excitements and dismays. Inside this
ring is another ring. This is a place where you sense your
ignorances, your unawarenesses, your inadequacies. Here is
where you are sorely tried, for this is your human self. And
so these rings get smaller as you near the center where you
find a place in you that longs for peace, calmness and spiritual
understanding. Finally there is the center which seems to the
imagination within a very small circumference. Here is

where you are, here is a place where you decide; here is where you are yourself. Most people seldom find it except in great moments; and yet when found and realized it encircles the universe. This is the quietness, this is the peace promised to those who seek. For this center lifts you high and clear of all the rings into eternal omniscient vision; here, when your mind is fastened to it and all your thoughts and all desires are pointed toward it, is the Spirit that will lead you through the valleys of the shadows of death, violence and hates and all the confusion that beset you and your country and your world at this time.

Hold to this center. You can only reach it in silence, you can only keep it in quietness, you can only feel it in serenity; this is the place of the pearl of great price. Carry the silence of your guarded center with you, guarded by the thoughts you have accepted. This is the way of a son of God. Every man in ordinary life presents a character which is instantly felt; everyone is revealed sooner or later, the vagaries of the human personality betray us. But the quietness of the realm I speak of is a steadying strength not of our making though of our accepting, and what is given forth from it is felt also. Remember always to acknowledge this; "of myself I can do nothing." What you have done is to seek the kingdom and having found it your task is to hold it, and that is a task indeed, for emotions, personalities can steal you away out among the outer rings; your thoughts, instead of being pointed toward your center race away into the mad dance.

Come back, come back and in holy stillness be lifted high above all this! Your dominion over yourself and the circumstances of your life can be glorious if you will keep your center clean, illumined and still in immortal silence. Here is selflessness, here is revealed true knowledge, wisdom, power and courage; the dignity of courage which is loyal to that which is not your human self. You will be given divine strategy in dealing with seemingly hopeless difficulties. The hates, criticisms, annoyances, the instinctive dislikes . . . keep them in the outer circumference. Turn your face away, turn it within toward that which is shining there. This is the kingdom of heaven. This is the task most needed now for yourself, for your loved ones, for your time. Each one anchored in this omnipotent stillness strengthens the soul of your nation.

"I never leave thee nor forsake thee, thou are in my keeping."

✍

DOWN THE AGES MAN HAS ATTEMPTED THROUGH THE discipline of monastic orders, hermitage and certain severe retirements from the world, to hold his half-awakened consciousness to the nearness of the presence of that which beats his heart and gives him life, gives him Life. Naked you are born, naked you die; it is seldom realized that naked and defenseless you live. Your defenselessness, humanly speaking, is exposed nakedly to a thousand dangers seen and unseen. A draught of air can dissolve you into eternity; and hatred, hidden and lodged deep within, can fester and destroy you. All these you can multiply for yourself. As a human you have no grip on life, however strong, healthy and outwardly protected you may be. Your only safety, fortress and eternal protection is your realization of the nearness of the presence of the Spirit; then you are clothed in the Spirit and are not naked. And by abiding in the Spirit, old ignorances are brought to the surface and released and you are made aware of those seeds of destruction within. These are your delayers and why it has taken you so long. If you had retired into a monastic life and given over your vigilance to others to keep for you in an ordered existence, regimented so that your emotional nature would be lulled by routine, you would have attained a peace of a secondary plane; these planes have their purpose, but you, who have chosen the difficult task, are healthier because you have asked for realization of the nearness and the actuality of the Spirit within, in a worldly, distracting, confusing life of alarms, of shocks, changes, stupidities and challenging despairs. You know that you are naked and defenseless. You stand alone with your desire to be at-one-with, to be aware of, to be *in* the Presence, while at the same time you must deal with the interruptions and delays, the temptations and appetites which, indulged in, act like sleeping draughts.

I tell you that the Spirit can overcome the sword and pain and sorrow; the Spirit *completely realized* will guide and protect you and lead you through all dangers; it will give you strength, power and inward peace. This is the reward of eternal vigilance, of the realization of him as your companion.

Be sanctified, be unbound, be free, be purified and aware of the Spirit, of love and joy, power and protection. Do not be the foolish ones who, in the bright sunlight, walketh and standeth in the dark tunnel and forget the light, and cannot picture it. Arise and come forth out of your restricted human life, here and now, and when you are by yourselves say these words:

"I open the doors of my heart wide knowing that the everlasting fountain of Thy light will pour forth and fill my life. I will be vigilant in guarding these doors that they shall not close of themselves because of my forgetfulness. I rest here with my heart open to receive, knowing that I am in the center of all things. I rest in gratitude and thanksgiving that the Spirit has filled this heart as a spring to break open and pour forth into my world. I will not let my heart be gripped by alarms and fears; it shall not be shut by violence and any untoward event. My sole intent is to keep these doors open for my very life's sake for I believe that out of the issues of my heart I shall be guided upon my journey and I shall be given strength."

O make in me those civil wars to cease!
Sir Philip Sidney, 1554-1586

What means fast, then? "Lo, this is the fast which I have chosen, saith the Lord. Loose every band of wickedness."
St. Clement of Alexandria, A.D. 150-220

Who would decline a sacrifice if once his soul had been accosted, his virtue recognized, and he was assured that a Watcher, a Holy One followed him ever with long affectionate glances of inexhaustible love?
Emerson's *Journal*

WHEN YOU SIT IN SILENCE IT IS AS IF YOU WERE IN AN ocean, vast, imperceptible, mysterious, so much is big and beyond you; and yet the mind of man, dwelling as it does in the elements, through desire, concentration and meditation has been inspired from within to touch the unseen Principle in some of its many manifestations. A turbine engine, a watch, all such ordered evidences are witnesses of the unseen. Man using his mind as an instrument has dipped into the ocean of the unseen around him, and has out of this made visible and practical the machines to make his life more comfortable. Forever and forever he puts his faith in that which he has made, forgetting that it is but a small part of the great oneness from which we can get everything we need. *There* is power; *there* is health; *there* is joy and knowledge and wisdom.

However great the storm, in the center of that ocean there is peace and life itself; all that you need as a son of God. So shape your desire and live as his son.

Man has instinctively known there is a beneficent quality in the living Principle within him because it has revealed itself in man's growth toward light. Therefore if it is essentially a principle of order, of rightness in all manifestations of material life, it is reasonable to assume that with confidence and an acceptance of the idea-Principle as perfect harmony, it is your business to make it your own. You can leave confusion behind and bathe your maladjustment in the Light that will heal it.

This conflict is beyond your human everyday understanding. It is partly the removal of much disease and ignorance. Suffice it for you to be undismayed, trusting to the beneficent Principle in the hearts of men who are now recognizing it swiftly; those who are in the realization of its power will be protected and give great things to the world. This is a time of crisis and both your lacks and spiritual fulfillments are being revealed. So fill yourselves with Light, stay in it, manifest it in your bodies, dip into this ocean with your lack and fill it! Do not accept the concepts of old age, disease and pain. Be in the vanguard of the great changes in the great days of crises. Out with these old ideas, and vibrate to the iron string that has been struck and say, "I am free from stagnation, I am an open clear channel, knowing that courage and faith will be given me when I stand in the protection of the eternal immortal present as a son of God!"

> *By faith . . . he endured as seeing Him who is invisible.*
>
> *Hebrews 11:27*

*For behold the Word, which is the Wisdom of God, is
in thy heart as a Light unto thy feet and lanthorn
unto thy paths. It is there as a speaking Word of God
in thy soul; and as soon as thou art ready to hear, this
eternal speaking Word will speak Wisdom and Love
in thy inward parts and bring forth the birth of
Christ, with all His holy nature, spirit and tempers,
within thee. Hence it was that so many eminent
spirits, partakers of the Divine Life have appeared in
so many parts of the heathen world; glorious names,
as lights hung out by God. . . . These were the
apostles of a Christ within.*

William Law, 1686-1761

ৎ

IN THE EFFORT TO STRUGGLE WITH HUMAN OBSTRUCTIONS,
feelings and thoughts, *your* thoughts and feelings take on
the heaviness of their human origin. That is the difficulty
of the life of human effort, that is what makes fatigue and
despondency and eventually becomes a physical handicap.
It is these heavy thoughts that soil you. These communions
restore you because during the time of your quiet receiving
from the source of the Spirit, you are bathed in the waters of
life. This will keep you pure in heart and your bodies sweet
with the Spirit; so illumined that you will not be fouled in
the mire of human living.

Therefore when effort is required of you in an endeavor
which calls for high intelligence, give it to the Spirit within
you to do, let him within you do the work as you were told,
and you will pass among the heavy, selfish, material lives
untouched and you will not be soiled and your body and your
spirit will be protected and forever refreshed. You will not
then have reactions, because the world will not have dominion
over you.

This is the mystery of the sacrament of living waters of baptism, daily baptism. Even in your daily bathing it would be healing for you to take it as a symbol of cleansing your spiritual body so that the presentment of your living self will be an inspiration of living purity. All that you have ever been told, all that you have sensed of the Spirit is reduced to the simple instruction . . . keep in touch with your divine companion in all the ways of your life.

We understand the power of materialism, we understand the morning hope you light your candle from, the Light of Ages within you. You go forth into material life and lo, the light of the candle is blown out and forgotten by the impact of this startling world of realities, so hard and bright.

Then coming home at night you cannot find the way to light so as to reillumine the candle because you are full of the thoughts that have been superimposed, that have darkened the child of the Spirit that started out so hopefully. Some of you say, "Is the lesson ever learned? Must I always begin at the beginning? Here I receive surcease, here comfort is restored, here I bathe in full lighted inspiration—to be rolled in the mire of material conflict . . ."

I tell you, each time a little more is gained, a little more is realized, a little more is made part of the regeneration. It is a mighty task, and yet it is the simplest. Now that the winds of calamity and despair are blowing in all directions, aside from the personal, insistent life of your foreground, you are challenged even more to be spiritually vigilant in your constant awareness. But your Comforter is not of this world, and never leaves nor forsakes you. Oh listen, listen, listen all the day through!

Though Christ a thousand times in Bethlehm be born,
And not within thyself, thy soul will be forlorn.
                              Pamela Grey, b. 1871

Clouded and shrouded there doth sit
The Infinite
Embosomed in a man; . . .
Then bear thyself, O man!
Up to the scale and compass of thy Guest;
. . . Be great as doth beseem
The ambassador who bears
The royal Presence where he goes.

Emerson's *Journal*

For the spiritual life is as much its own proof as the natural life, and needs no outward or foreign thing to bear witness to it.

William Law 1686

The tendency of modern physics is to resolve the whole material universe into waves and nothing but waves; these are waves of two kinds; bottled up waves which we call matter and unbottled waves which we call radiation or light. If annihilation of matter occurs, the process is merely that of unbottling imprisoned wave energy and letting it fall to travel through space. These concepts reduce the whole universe to a world of light, potential and existent, so that the whole story of creation can be told with perfect accuracy and completeness in the six words, "God said, 'Let there be light.'"

Sir James Jeans, 1877 ——

He that wonders shall reign; and he that reigns shall rest.
Look with wonder at that which is before you.

Traditional Sayings of Jesus,
St. Clement of Alexandria, A.D. 150-220

My mystery is for me and the sons of my house.

Traditional Sayings of Jesus,
St. Clement of Alexandria, A.D. 150-220

Jesus saith, Wherever . . . there is one . . . alone I am with him. Raise the stone and there thou shalt find me, cleave the wood and there am I.

The Logia Jesu, taken from an early Greek papyrus
dated A.D. 150-300, found at Oxyrhynchus, 1897

. . . I receive, in proportion to my obedience, truth from God; I put myself aside and let Him be.

Emerson's *Journal*

, ... Refrain tonight;
And that shall lend a kind of easiness
To the next abstinence: the next more easy;
For use almost can change the stamp of nature,
And master ev'n the devil or throw him out
With wondrous potency.

Hamlet, Act III Scene IV
Shakespeare

It is by yourself without ambassador that God speaks to you. You are as one who has a private door that leads him to the king's chamber.

Emerson's *Journal*

I will rejoice that from all tormenting we can retreat always upon the Invisible Heart, upon the Celestial Love, and that not to be soothed merely, but to be replenished, not to be compensated, but to receive power to make all things new.

Emerson. From a Letter